mustsees
Vancouver

BC Place Stadium and False Creek/©Chris Cheadle/age fotostock

mustsees **Vancouver**

Editorial Director	Cynthia Clayton Ochterbeck
Editorial Manager	Gwen Cannon
Writers	Pamela Delaney, Eric Lucas
Production Manager	Natasha G. George
Cartography	Peter Wrenn
Photo Researcher	Nicole D. Jordan
Layout	Nicole D. Jordan
Additional Layout	Natasha G. George
Cover & Interior Design	Chris Bell, cbdesign
Cover Design & Layout	Natasha G. George

Contact Us

Michelin Travel and Lifestyle North America
One Parkway South
Greenville, SC 29615, USA
travel.lifestyle@us.michelin.com
www.michelintravel.com

Michelin Travel Partner
Hannay House
39 Clarendon Road
Watford, Herts WD17 1JA, UK
www.ViaMichelin.com
travelpubsales@uk.michelin.com

Special Sales

For information regarding bulk sales, customized
editions and premium sales, please contact us at:
travel.lifestyle@us.michelin.com
www.michelintravel.com

Michelin Travel Partner

Société par actions simplifiées au capital de 11 629 590 EUR
27 cours de l'Ile Seguin - 92100 Boulogne Billancourt (France)
R.C.S. Nanterre 433 677 721

© 2013 Michelin Travel Partner
ISBN 978-2-067182-05-9
Printed: November 2012
Printed and bound in Italy

Note to the reader:
While every effort is made to ensure that all information printed in this guide is correct
and up-to-date, Michelin Travel Partner accepts no liability for any direct, indirect or
consequential losses howsoever caused so far as such can be excluded by law. Admission
prices listed for sights in this guide are for a single adult, unless otherwise specified.

©City of Vancouver

Introduction

Must See

p 79

p 110

©Harbour Cruises Ltd.

Must Do

Must Eat

Must Stay

Must Know

TABLE OF CONTENTS

5

★★★ ATTRACTIONS

Unmissable historic, cultural and natural sights

©City of Vancouver

Stanley Park p 64

©Royal BC Museum

Royal British Columbia Museum (Old Town exhibit) p 87

©Leslie Forsberg/Michelin

UBC Museum of Anthropology (Haida Bear (1963) by Bill Reid) p 52

Pacific Rim National Park Reserve (Long Beach) p 94

©Dededa/age fotostock

Vancouver Aquarium (Penguin Point) p 114

©Meighan Makarchuk/Vancouver Aquarium

Butchart Gardens (Ross Fountain) p 93

Courtesy of The Butchart Gardens

★★★ ATTRACTIONS

Unmissable historic, cultural and natural sights

For more than 75 years people have used Michelin stars to take the guesswork out of travel. Our star-rating system helps you make the best decision on where to go, what to do, and what to see.

★★★	Unmissable
★★	Worth a trip
★	Worth a detour
No star	Recommended

MUST KNOW

ACTIVITIES

Vancouver's awesome setting and abundant opportunities for recreation enliven city life to the nth degree. We recommend every activity in this guide, but the Michelin Man logo highlights our top picks.

Outings

Hotels

Shows

Relax

Restaurants

Shopping

Side Trips

Sports

STAR ATTRACTIONS

IDEAS AND TOURS

Throughout this thematic guide you will find inspiration for many different ways to experience Vancouver and its surroundings. The following is a selection of places and activities from the guide to help start you off. The sights in bold are found in the index.

Fishing and Hunting

In British Columbia fishing ranges from **deep-sea** pursuit of large salmon and halibut to backcountry **fly-fishing** for indigenous wilderness trout. Key species are chinook, coho, sockeye and pink salmon, as well as rainbow and cutthroat trout. Some fishing excursions are available from **Vancouver★★★** and **Victoria★★★**, most of which are day or half-day trips, but wilderness expeditions are popular, and often use these major cities as their base. Overnight stays at ranches and wilderness lodges with fishing facilities are possible. For example, **Big Bar Ranch** *(877-655-2333; www.bigbarranch.com)*, a 6hr drive northeast of Vancouver, provides fishing equipment for its nearby trout-filled lakes.

Nonresidents must obtain a licence, available from sporting-goods stores. For information on seasons, catch and possession limits, visit www.envgov. bc.ca/fw/wildlife or www.env.gov. bc.ca/fw/fish. For information on fishing and hunting trips around Vancouver, Victoria and Whistler, and licence fees, as well as listings of outfitters, contact the **Guide Outfitters Association of BC** at www.goabc.org.

Golf

Because of its climate, southern British Columbia offers one of the longest seasons for golfing in Canada. Vancouver's **Fraserview, Langara** and **McCleery** golf courses as well as putting greens in Stanley Park and Queen Elizabeth Park are run by the city parks and recreation office *(vancouver.ca)* In **Whistler★★★** world-class courses *(www.golfwhistler.com)* such as **Château Whistler Golf Club, Nicklaus North** and **Whistler Golf Club** were designed by top-notch golfers. Some greens afford ocean and mountain views, and many facilities feature local cuisine and wines. To locate golf facilities in Vancouver and on Vancouver Island, visit www.hellobc.com or www.britishcolumbiagolf.org.

Hiking and Walking

BC has thousands of miles of hiking trails, ranging from urban paths skirting the Vancouver waterfront to wilderness routes that take weeks to traverse. The **West Coast Trail** is a legendary trek along the edge of southwest Vancouver Island through deep forests, thick mud, rocky headlands amid temperamental weather; it is part of **Pacific Rim National Park★★★** *(www.pc.gc.ca)*. Less taxing is the **Juan de Fuca Trail** to the south.

In Vancouver proper, walking is a pleasure, be it through the varied topography and features of **Stanley Park★★★** or along the newer seawall that connected various facilities for the 2010 Vancouver Olympics. **Lighthouse**

MUST KNOW

Park★★ on the North Shore has several trails to the lighthouse, a great place to see the sun set. Despite its size, Vancouver is a city made for walkers; downtown neighbourhoods are condensed and historic sites abound. Walking tours can be done solo with the aid of a good map, or as guided group expeditions to landmarks of the past.

International Travel Maps (*www.itmb.com*) offers a large range of maps at its Richmond store. Mountain Equipment Co-op, Canada's REI, has an extensive selection of maps at its stores (*www.mec.ca*).

Riding

Horseback riding opportunities range from hour-long trail rides to one-week or longer excursions. Trails are located in regions just outside BC's two major cities, and all around Whistler. **Sundance Guest Ranch** (*800-553-3533; www.sundanceguestranch.com*), a 4hr drive northeast of Vancouver, is perched above the Thompson River near Ashcroft; the resort offers tennis courts, a heated pool and trail rides as well as overnight stays in rustic rooms. BC's oldest ranch, the **Flying U Ranch** (*877-456-7717; www.flyingu.com*) lies 5hrs northeast of Vancouver; here guests saddle their own horses and follow trails with trail map in hand. Contact BC Tourism for information about the many riding opportunities and outfitters in the province (*www. hellobc.com*). For information on equestrian events, contact Equine Canada (*www.canadaequine.com*).

Skiing and Boarding

With a dozen major destination resorts—and three ski areas just outside Vancouver—British Columbia is a North American ski capital that compares to Colorado. Onshore Pacific weather flows bring dependable snowfall, often in large amounts. Along Vancouver's North Shore, not far from downtown, **Mount Seymour, Grouse Mountain★★** and **Cypress Mountain** offer skiers ready access and prodigious snowfalls (*Nov-Mar*). All three alpine ski areas offer lighted skiing at night. World-famed, **Whistler★★★** is

©Eric P. Lucas/Michelin

Cross-country skiing in the Whistler area

Kayaks, False Creek

©City of Vancouver

often the top-ranked ski resort on earth by ski magazines; its slopes and venues were home to many of the events in the 2010 Vancouver Olympics. Its mountain-base village offers world-class lodging for more than 10,000 visitors, and its two vast mountains constitute the biggest single skiing complex on the continent. Skiing begins at Whistler each year in early November and winds up the season in June; this long season enables skiers to hit the slopes on a brisk May morning, and tee off at a golf course that afternoon. For a complete rundown on BC ski resorts, visit *www.hellobc.com*.

Water Sports

British Columbia holds several of the world's best-known water sports locales, including canoeing and kayaking in and around Vancouver and Victoria. Mountain rivers and lakes provide ideal spots in the wilderness around Whistler, too. Because BC has such a lengthy coastline, and a mixture of ocean and inland waterways, the options are virtually limitless.

Saltwater **Desolation Sound**, north of Vancouver, and **Barkley Sound**, south of Ucluelet on the west coast of Vancouver Island, are famed worldwide among sea kayakers. Both comprise innumerable islands and coves to explore, with hidden sand beaches and, in Desolation Sound, unusually warm waters in late summer. If your passion is the freedom and intimacy of kayaking, be sure to visit **Clayoquot Sound** and Broughton Archipelago. Barkley Sound is part of Pacific Rim National Park; for information visit www.pc.gc.ca.

Canoes and kayaks are available for rent at many points, ranging from downtown Vancouver at **English Bay** to the Inner harbour at Victoria (visit www.vancouverisland.com/kayaking for more information). Experience the rush of **whitewater** kayaking on the buoyant rivers of Vancouver Island. For trip planning and information, visit www.paddlecanada.com and www.canoekayak.ca.

Wildlife Watching

Visitors to the province regularly see bears, beavers, deer, moose, caribou and other woodland fauna; as well as whales, bald eagles, seals, sea lions and numerous other shore creatures. Such wildlife is not abundant on downtown Vancouver streets, obviously, but wild animals might be encountered in city-based locales such as **Stanley Park**.

Wildlife-watching adventures depart from Vancouver and Victoria, by road or by water, to take camera buffs and nature lovers on day-long outings within short range of these major cities. The northern section of **Georgia Strait** is renowned for its whale-watching, though controversy is growing over the practice, which causes great disturbance for the whales. For information about Canadian wildlife, visit the **Canadian Wildlife Federation's** website: www.cwf-fcf.org or call them at 800-563-9453, and **Environment Canada's** website at www.ec.gc.ca. Wildlife is best observed in the province's provincial and national parks, although thousands of visitors are astounded to discover bears, moose, elk and other large animals simply browsing the roadside vegetation along highways in the interior and on Vancouver Island. When watching or photographing wildlife, a respectful distance is crucial. It is illegal and inappropriate, not to mention highly dangerous, to interact with wild animals in any way, especially feeding them. Wildlife advocates argue that any human action that causes wild animals to change their behaviour is wrong. Stiff fines are given in parks for feeding and otherwise habituating wildlife: never feed, pet or disturb wild creatures of any kind. Large animals such as bears and moose can be extremely dangerous.

Farms and Markets

A large swath of the land around urban centres in BC hosts farms. In fact, the **Okanagan Valley★★** and rural areas around Vancouver form the western branch of Canada's three main "bread

©Leslie Forsberg/Michelin

Great Blue Heron

baskets," together with the Niagara Peninsula, centrally located in Ontario, and the Annapolis Valley of Nova Scotia on the east coast. BC farmers commonly sell their fresh, and sometimes organic, produce, dairy products and meats through collective farm markets or directly from their farms. Not only does a farm market tour remind participants of where food comes from (hint: not the supermarket), but it results in a cache of delicious edibles for the trip home. Visit the **Fraser Valley**, Okanagan Valley and **Vancouver Island** for farms abundant with the good things in life, a tasty way to be educated and entertained. Find more information and a farm tour plan by visiting www.circlefarmtour. com. Note: most farms and farm markets sell on a seasonal basis. Visit www.hellobc.com for more information. If you can't manage to get out of town for a few hours or a day, let the farmers come to you; Vancouver and Victoria both have excellent city-based farmers'

markets, the best of which is year-round on **Granville Island★★**; visit www.granvilleisland.com for details.

Spas
See Spas.

The spa retreat has become a popular getaway vacation in Vancouver, Victoria and Whistler. Some of Vancouver's long-established beauty/therapeutic and medical spas helped create the Canadian spa industry, and continue to expand its horizons by incorporating new treatments based on locally available herbs and other botanicals, as well as treatments entrenched in native practice.

Most major urban hotels incorporate day spas among their facilities; fees vary according to the treatments requested. Many are located in Vancouver or Victoria proper or within an hour's drive from each; both cities are resplendent with day spas.

Spa retreats are found in sublime

Cherry Point Vineyards, Cobble Hill

©Cherry Point Estate Wines

non-urban locales, typically set amid spectacular scenery, and are often included as part of larger resorts such as ranches or wilderness lodges.

Echo Valley Ranch and Spa
(800-253-8831; www.evranch. com) lies 270mi northeast of Vancouver via Whistler or Fraser Canyon routes. Overnight guests choose from a variety of Asian spa treatments at the full-service spa. For a list of BC destination spas, visit www.hellobc.com.

Wineries

See BC Wine Country and Cowichan Valley. With about 200 wineries—many within an hour or two by car from Vancouver—this area has become a major and seriously recognized New World wine region. From big-output winery production facilities to small family-run vineyards with limited vintages, the choices are vast and varied. The combination of diverse, award-winning wines, stunning scenery and the laid-back sensibility of BC wine regions makes for a pleasurable day of sampling. To ensure you don't mix sipping and driving, local operators offer guided tours in buses. Visit www.hellobc.com for more information or to participate in an **Okanagan Valley★★** winery tour, visit www.okwinetours. com. A great way to enjoy winery expeditions is to tour the vineyards during the day and find a perfect restaurant in the city for dinner that night, one with a wine list that focuses on local vintages.

Quick Trips

Stuck for ideas? Try these:

IDEAS AND TOURS

CALENDAR OF EVENTS

Listed below are the most popular events in the Vancouver area, including Vancouver Island. Dates are subject to change. For the most current information, contact **Tourism Vancouver** (*604-682-2222; www. tourismvancouver.com*); **Tourism Victoria** (*250-953-2033; www.tourism victoria.com*); and **Tourism BC** (*800-435-5622; www.hellobc.com*).

January

Chinese New Year Festival
604-662-3207. Chinatown, www.cbavancouver.ca
In Vancouver, the Chinese Benevolent Association celebrates with a colourful parade to toast the new year. Some 50,000 people watch marching bands, dancers, martial artists and floats.

February

BC Home & Garden Show
604-639-2288, BC Place Stadium, www.bchomeandgarden show.com
This show offers hands-on fun for every aspect of home life. HGTV stars take to the stage for witty talks on making the most of your domicile.

Vancouver International Boat Show
604-678-8820, BC Place and Granville Island, www.vancouverboatshow.ca

Now expanded to include an in-water venue (the marina at Granville Island), the show is designed to awe and inform, with new boats on display, new products to make boating and sailing safer, and seminars that help experienced and novice sailors get into the groove. There are even boat rides to inspire future sailors.

Vancouver International Comedy Festival
See Performing Arts.

Vancouver International Wine Festival
604-872-6623, Former Vancouver Playhouse, www.vanwinefest.ca
Almost 800 wines from some 200 wineries in 15 countries. Attendees enjoy tastings, wine dinners and wine seminars.

March

Pacific Rim Whale Festival
250-725-3414, Tofino, Ucluelet, www.pacificrimwhalefestival.com
The focus is watching gray whales, but events include the annual Gala Dinner and Silent Auction at the Wickaninnish Inn.

Vancouver International Dance Festival
604-662-7441, Various venues, www.vidf.ca
VIDF offers classical ballet to interpretative performances by individuals and troupes. Adjuncts include an art exhibit and dance workshops.

March: Pacific Rim Whale Festival

©Marilyn McEwen

April

Vancouver Sun Run 10k
604-689-9441, Downtown.
www.vancouversun.com/sunrun
This 10km road race is not technically a charity event, but it has donated millions to amateur athletics and national literacy. In 2011, 60,000 participants made it the largest event of its kind in the world.

World Ski & Snowboard Festival
604-938-3399, Whistler,
www.wssf.com
This winter-sports event has fashion shows, outdoor concerts, a film and photography showdown, a "silent" disco (dance to music delivered through headphones), and a dog parade.

May

Swiftsure International Yacht Race
250-592-9098, Victoria Inner Harbour, www.swiftsure.org
This prestigious yacht race, hosted by the Royal Victoria Yacht Club, is for sailors with the experience to negotiate the rugged coastline of the Juan de

May
Vancouver
International
Children's
Festival

©Tim Matheson

Fuca Strait. The event holds three overnight races comprising 80, 103 and 139 nautical miles, and a single-day course.

Vancouver International Children's Festival
See For Kids.

June

Bard on the Beach
See Performing Arts.

Comox Shellfish Festival
250-890-7561, Comox,
www.bcshellfishfestival.ca
Enter the oyster-shucking contest or chowder challenge, or watch a shellfish cooking

©Richard Lam

The Vancouver Sun Run

demonstration. Booths offer wares from hand-crafted jewellery to produce.

Dragon Boat Festival
604-688-2382, False Creek,
www.dragonboatbc.ca
This popular summer event mixes thunderous drums, team spirit and music. Teams of dragon boats are put together, often within the corporate culture and mostly with a charitable undercurrent.

Vancouver International Jazz Festival
See Performing Arts.

Vancouver Storytelling Festival
604-876-2272, Various venues,
www.vancouverstorytelling.org
Occurs every other year.
This festival, held every other year, was founded by Vancouver area librarians. It regains the traditional hold on telling stories as established long ago by Native tribes in their longhouses. While there are numerous adjuncts to the festival, the sharing of stories is the magical focus.

July
Canada Day (July 1)
604-775-7200, Canada Place and Granville Island,
www.canadaday.canadaplace.ca
www.granvilleisland.com
Paint your face white and maple-leaf red and dance all day. Then watch fireworks at night as Canada celebrates another year.

Celebration of Light
See Performing Arts.

Theatre under the Stars
See Performing Arts.

Vancouver Folk Music Festival
See Performing Arts.

Vancouver Pride Week
604-687-0955, Various venues,
www.vancouverpride.ca
The Gay Pride parade is the highlight of Pride Week in Vancouver, and rainbows abound as the the LGBT community takes to the streets. There's even a Pride Beer for the occasion. Thousands of revellers watch the parade as it winds its way through the West End of the city.

August
MusicFest Vancouver
604-688-1152, Various venues,
www.musicfestvancouver.com
Featuring classical, jazz and world music, the festival spans 10 days and 40 venues. Acts include international stars the likes of the Carpe Diem String Quartet, American soprano Dawn Upshaw, Finland's vocal sensation Rajaton, the Danish National Girls Choir and everything in between.

Pacific National Exhibition
604-253-2311, Hastings Park (through Sept), www.pne.ca
The "PNE" opened in 1910 and has been established as one of North America's major annual

August MusicFest Vancouver

©MusicFest Vancouver

December: Festival of Lights

fairs since then. With midway rides and games, exhibits, seminars, horse and dog shows, and contests for the best in produce and livestock, it's a circus of fun to mark the end of summer.

September
Vancouver Fringe Festival
See Performing Arts.
Vancouver International Film Festival
See Performing Arts.

October
Vancouver International Writers & Readers Festival
604-681-6330, Granville Island, www.writersfest.bc.ca
Tributes to literary greats, readings by authors, and a celebration of ideas and written creativity mark this festival, a favourite of great Canadian writers (like Alistair MacLeod, Jane Urquhart and Margaret Atwood, for example) and fans.

November
Heritage Christmas
604-297-4565, Burnaby Village Museum (through Dec), www.burnabyvillagemuseum.ca
Stroll through the past in this re-created village; at the stunning festival, the "town" museum gets all decked out for a bygone-era celebration. Be sure to visit the archives, gift shop and gallery, but don't miss the carousel.

Vancouver Fashion Week
78-996-2200, Stanley Park Pavilion, www.vanfashionweek.com
Fashion designers from around the world and across the street merge during this week, showing everything from haute couture to streetwear, and all that lies in the folds between. The focus is, naturally, on local designers, but this event has become one of the most vital international fashion events on the Pacific Rim.

December
Festival of Lights
604-257-8335, VanDusen Botanical Garden, www.vandusengarden.org
Every branch, bloom and blade is decked out in lights at this glittering annual event. There are literally hundreds of thousands of lights in all colours sparkling in the dark as visitors stroll down Candy Cane Lane. Throughout the gardens can be heard the sweet sound of carollers. Kids can visit with Santa Claus and his elves.

PRACTICAL INFORMATION

WHEN TO GO

The main **tourist season** for most of Canada, including Vancouver and all of British Columbia, begins the last weekend in May (Victoria Day) through the first weekend in September (Labour Day). Travel is especially heavy in July and August. Many attractions extend the season to the Thanksgiving weekend (second Monday in October), though tourist crowds diminish considerably after Labour Day. From early April to mid-May, visitors can usually enjoy comfortable daytime temperatures but expect cool nights in the **spring**; light showers are likely. July, August and September are ideal for outdoor activities such as sailing, kayaking, canoeing or hiking. Warm, sunny days with temperatures ranging from 22°–25°C/70°–80°F characterize the **summer** months. Oddly enough, though it is surrounded by water, Vancouver experiences little humid weather in the summer. October can be the best month to visit, since the days remain sunny for the most part, and the deciduous trees put on a bright display.

For the sports enthusiast, **winter**, generally from mid-November to mid-March, offers excellent opportunities to enjoy downhill skiing, cross-country skiing, dogsledding, snowshoeing and snowmobiling. All these activities are possible both on Vancouver Island and on the mainland, most notably in Whistler (*see Excursions*).

KNOW BEFORE YOU GO

Before you go, contact the following organizations in and around Vancouver for information about sightseeing, accommodations, recreation and annual events.

Tourist Offices

Tourism Vancouver

www.tourismvancouver.com – 201-200 Burrard St., Vancouver, BC V6C 3L6 Canada. 604-683-2000.

Tourism BC

www.hellobc.com – British Columbia Visitor Centre @ Peace Arch, 298 Highway 99, Surrey, BC V3S 9N7 Canada. 800-HELLO-BC.

Tourism Victoria

www.tourismvictoria.com – 812 Wharf St., Victoria, BC V8W 1T3 Canada. 250-953-2033 or 800-663-3883.

Tourism Whistler

www.whistler.com – 4010 Whistler Way, Whistler, BC V0N 1B4 Canada. 604-932-3928 or 800-944-7853.

Average Seasonal Temperatures in Vancouver				
	Jan	**Apr**	**Jul**	**Oct**
Avg. High	6°C/43°F	13°C/55°F	22°C/72°F	14°C/57°F
Avg. Low	1°C/34°F	5°C/41°F	13°C/55°F	7°C/44°F

MUST KNOW

Visitor Centres

Tourism Vancouver
200 Burrard St., Plaza Level,
Vancouver.
*Open year-round daily
8:30am–6pm.*

Tourism Victoria
812 Wharf St., Victoria.
*Open May–Sept daily 8:30am–
8:30pm. Rest of the year daily
9am–5pm. Closed Dec. 25.*

Tourism Whistler
4230 Gateway Dr., Whistler.
Open year-round daily 8am–10pm.

Useful Websites
In addition to the official tourism
websites above, try these sites for
useful visitor information:

www.canada.com – Provides
local, regional and national features
on all things Canadian.

www.canoe.ca – The website of
a media provider offering news,
movie listings, sports, weather.

www.cbc.ca – Canadian
Broadcasting Corp.' website for
news, sports and entertainment.

www.pc.gc.ca – Parks Canada lists
all of the country's national parks.,
historic sites and areas.

www.vancouversun.com –
The city's leading daily newspaper,
which provides extensive coverage
of arts, entertainment and sports
in Vancouver.

**www.canada.com/the
province** – The *Vancouver Province*
is a tabloid that offers a down-to-
earth perspective on local affairs.

www.straight.com –
The Georgia Straight, the city's
alternative weekly, has the
most comprehensive arts and
entertainment coverage every
Wednesday.

www.cityfood.com – City Food
is a monthly devoted to restaurant
news and reviews.

www.xtra.ca – *Xtra West*, a free
weekly, covers the city's LGBT
scene.

www.weatheroffice.gc.ca –
Area weather forecasts from
Environment Canada.

INTERNATIONAL VISITORS
In addition to local tourism offices,
visitors may obtain information
from the nearest Canadian
embassy or consulate in their
country of residence. Embassies
of other countries are located in
Canada's capital, Ottawa. Many
foreign countries also maintain
consulates in Vancouver. For
further information on all Canadian
embassies and consulates abroad,
contact the website of the
Canadian Department of Foreign
Affairs and International Trade:
www.dfait-maeci.gc.ca.

Entry Requirements
Travellers from the US need a valid
(machine readable) **passport** to
visit Canada and return to the US
by air. Canadian and US citizens
must present a passport to cross
the Canada/US border by land
or sea. Requirements can and do
change; visit www.cbp.gov for the
latest information.

To bring children into Canada, single parents (whether divorced or simply unaccompanied by their spouse) travelling with children must bring a notarized permission letter from the other parent, as well as a passport or special enhanced ID.

Only a **passport** or other appropriate secure document will be accepted for anyone, including US citizens, to enter the US. Check the websites www.canada.travel or www.travel.state.gov (US government site) for the most recent updates. All other visitors to Canada must have a valid passport and in some cases, a visa (see list of countries at www.cic.gc.ca/english/visit/visas.asp). No vaccinations are necessary. For entry into Canada via the US, all persons or legal residents are required to present a valid passport or special US-issued border-crossing ID. Check with the Canadian embassy or consulate in your home country about entry regulations and proper travel documents.

Persons seeking entry to Canada who have ever been convicted of a crime (including marijuana possession) or, in some cases, have ever been arrested, should be aware that they may be denied entry. If you have any doubt, check with Canadian border authorities before heading to Canada.

Border Crossings

For entry into Canada via the US, all persons are required to present a valid **passport** or special government-issued enhanced ID designed for border crossing purposes. The US-Canada border crossing at Blaine is the busiest west of Michigan. Lines can grow long on weekends and holidays; the best time to cross, either way, is early morning weekdays and Sundays. It is much easier heading north into Canada, which has 10 lanes for border inspection, than returning to the US, which has just three lanes. When crossing the border, do not try to carry contraband. Don't take any weapons into Canada, or Cuban cigars into the States.

Canada Customs

Visitors over 19 years of age entering British Columbia (age 18 in some Canadian provinces) may bring 1.14 litres of liquor or 1.5 litres of wine or 24 cans of beer (totaling a maximum of 8.5 litres) without paying duty or taxes. Tobacco is limited to 200 cigarettes, 50 cigars or cigarillos, 200 tobacco sticks, or 200 grams/7oz of loose manufactured product. Gifts totalling $60 Canadian may be brought in duty-free. All prescription drugs should be clearly labeled and for personal use only; it's best to carry a copy of the prescription. For details, call the Border Information Service (800-467-9999, Vancouver) or write to Border Services Agency, Ottawa, Ontario, K1A 0L5 Canada (800-461-9999; www.cbsa-asfc.gc.ca). Canada has stringent legislation on firearms—do not bring any weapons to the border. For further information on entry of firearms, contact the Canadian Centre for Firearms (284 Wellington St., Ottawa, Ontario K1A 0H8 Canada; 800-731-4000; www.rcmp-grc.gc.ca/cfp-pcaf).

Driving in Canada

See Getting There, By Car, below.

GETTING THERE
By Air
Vancouver International Airport (YVR) is located 10km/7mi south of downtown (604-207-7077; www.yvr.ca). The airport services major domestic and international carriers, with nonstop flights from Asia, Europe and North America. Air Canada (888-247-2262; www.aircanada.com) and its affiliates provide connections to regions throughout the province.

Taxi service to downtown costs $35. Major car rental agencies are located at the airport.

A great way to get to the airport is via the Canada Line **SkyTrain**; it travels from the airport to downtown in 26 minutes (http://tripplanning.translink.ca/hiwire?.a=iScheduleLookupSearch&LineName=999&LineAbbr=999).

Airport Fees
Upon departure from some Canadian cities, travellers should be prepared to pay in cash an **Airport Improvement Fee**; in Vancouver, departing passengers flying within British Columbia pay $5, and those flying out of the province pay $20.

By Train
Daily service to Pacific Central Station at the east end of downtown (1150 Station St.) is provided by **VIA Rail**. Canada's national passenger service, VIA Rail links major cities within the country. In Canada, consult the telephone directory for the nearest office or call 888-842-7245 or go online (www.viarail.ca).

This station is also the terminal for **Amtrak** service from the US (800-872-7245; www.amtrak.com).

By Bus
Pacific Central Station (1150 Station St.) is Vancouver's departure point for all buses. For travel from the US or within Canada, contact **Greyhound** (604-683-8133 or 800-661-8747; www.greyhound.ca).

By Car
Vancouver lies at the westernmost end of the Fraser River Valley in southwestern BC. The main highway access from the east is Highway 1, the Trans-Canada Highway. From the south, access is along Highway 99, which becomes Interstate 5 when it crosses into the US at the Blaine border crossing. Drivers from the US may use valid state-issued licences. Visitors from elsewhere should obtain an International Driving Permit through their national automobile association in order to rent a car. Drivers must carry vehicle registration and/or rental contract, and proof of automobile insurance at all times. Gasoline is sold by the litre. Vehicles in Canada are driven on the right-hand side of the road.

Car Rental Companies
+ **Alamo** – 800-327-9633 www.alamo.com.
+ **Avis** – 800-331-1212 www.avis.com.
+ **Budget** – 800-527-0700 www.budget.com.
+ **Dollar** – 800-800-4000 www.dollar.com.
+ **Enterprise**– 800-325-8007 www.enterprise.com.
+ **Hertz** – 800-654-3131 www.hertz.com.
+ **National** – 800-227-7368 www.nationalcar.com.
+ **Thrifty** – 800-331-4200 www.thrifty.com.

PRACTICAL INFORMATION

GETTING AROUND
Orientation

Downtown Vancouver sits on a small peninsula bordered by saltwater inlets on both sides, with Stanley Park at the northwest end. Most of Vancouver's downtown city streets are laid out in a **grid pattern,** with streets running southeast-northwest and northeast-southwest. The main downtown arteries are Granville, Burrard and Denman streets, running northeast to southwest; and Davie and Georgia streets, running southeast to northwest. Georgia Street is the thoroughfare that leads to the Lions Gate Bridge, heading to the North Shore; Granville and Burrard streets cross their namesake bridges over False Creek heading south.

To the southwest, walking and cycle paths run from the beaches of English Bay around False Creek and on to Kitsilano. The West End is largely residential. Yaletown's new residential towers line False Creek. Avoid East Hastings Street area (*see On Foot*).

On Foot

Vancouver is best seen on foot. Most downtown sights can be reached within a half hour (or less) from major hotels; from Stanley Park, at one end of downtown, to Chinatown at the other, is a 30-minute walk. (Do not walk along **East Hastings Street,** a drug district.) Street numbers rise as you go westward and northward; even numbers are on the east or north sides of the street.

By Car

Vancouver's **rush hour** extends from 7:30am–9am, and 4pm–6pm, but it is mild by North American urban standards. On the other hand, some streets, such as South Granville, are likely to be congested any time between 6am and 10pm. **Speed limits**, posted in kilometres, are generally 100km/h (60mph) on freeways, 90km/h (55mph) on the Trans-Canada routes, and 80km/h (50mph) on most highways. The speed limit in cities and towns slows to 50km/h (30mph).

Headlights must be turned on at all times. The use of seat belts is mandatory. Parking spaces on downtown streets are limited, and parking regulations are strictly enforced. Limited metered parking is available on non-arterial streets, and parking lots and garages are plentiful. Posted rush-hour restrictions generally prohibit parking and stopping 7am–9am and 4:30pm–6pm (times vary).

Parking

Parking signs are colour-coded: green-and-white signs indicate hours when parking is allowed; red-and-white signs indicate hours when parking is not allowed. Stopping during restricted times could result in your vehicle being towed. Parking spaces identified with a handicapped symbol are reserved for people with disabilities.

By Public Transportation

TransLink *(604-953-3333; www.translink.bc.ca)* operates an extensive system of public buses, ferries **(SeaBus)** and light rail lines **(SkyTrain, West Coast Express)** in Vancouver. Hours of operation are: Mon–Sat 6am–1:30am, Sun

Traffic on Burrard Street Bridge

©City of Vancouver

9am–1:30am. Adult fares one-way range from $2.50–$5 (exact fare required; drivers do not sell tickets). A **Day Pass**, good for unlimited one-day travel, is $8. Transfers are free between buses, public ferries and light rail. System maps and timetables are available free of charge.

By Taxi

Numerous taxi companies operate in the city under municipal licensing supervision—drivers must demonstrate knowledge of English, be courteous and prove their familiarity with the city. When the "Taxi" sign on the roof of the cab is lit, the vehicle is available for hire. Most downtown runs cost $10–$15 (on average $1.92/km); from downtown to the airport costs about $35. Vancouver's major taxi companies include **Yellow Cab** (604-681-1111) and **Black Top Cabs** (604-681-2181). **McLure's Cabs** have been serving Vancouver since 1911 (604-696-8838).

By Ferry

See below.

GETTING TO VANCOUVER ISLAND AND VICTORIA

Even though Highway 1 starts in Victoria (and goes all the way to the island of Newfoundland), you can't just drive there—the Strait of Georgia intervenes. That's why thousands of people hop in their vehicles early on Friday afternoons to get in line for ferry passage to Vancouver Island. The bad news is, there are thousands of those island-hoppers; the good news is, advance planning and flexibility will allow you to bypass the worst of the crush.

By Ferry

BC Ferries, the province's ferry service, operates three runs to the island from the Vancouver area (888-223-3779; www.bcferries.com). The Tsawwassen terminal south of the city (follow Granville St. south to Hwy. 99) serves ferries crossing to both Swartz Bay (Victoria) and Duke Point (Nanaimo and the rest of the island). The Horseshoe Bay terminal in West Vancouver (at the continental end of Hwy. 1, take Georgia St.

west across the Lions Gate Bridge) serves ferries to Nanaimo, as well as other destinations. All three runs to the island consist of large boats departing roughly every two hours. Once you reach the island, it's about a half-hour drive into downtown **Victoria** from Swartz Bay; and three hours from Nanaimo to Tofino. Passage for a vehicle and driver varies by season and day, but peaks at about $35. To beat the crowds, make an advance reservation. The ferries' reserved boarding service carries a premium—$15 one way— but it's worth it.

By Air

Several airline operations fly between Vancouver and the island. The two most popular airlines both depart from downtown sites near Canada Place.

Helijet (800-665-4354; www.helijet.com) flies Bell Jet Ranger craft to a landing pad at the entrance to Victoria's inner harbour. Passage takes about 25 minutes; the view of the Gulf Islands is wonderful.

Harbour Air (departs from downtown floatplane base just west of Canada Place; 800-665-0212; www.harbour-air.com) flies floatplanes—mostly the de Havilland Beavers and Otters that are considered some of the sturdiest planes ever built. Passage to Victoria takes about 40 minutes.

ACCESSIBILITY

Most public buildings, public transit and ferries, and many attractions, restaurants and hotels in Vancouver provide **wheelchair access**. Disabled parking is provided and the law is strictly enforced. For details, contact Tourism Vancouver. Many national and provincial parks have restrooms and other facilities for the disabled (such as wheelchair-accessible nature trails or tour buses). For details about a specific park, call 888-773-8888 or check online at www.pc.gc.ca. Passengers who will need special assistance with train travel should contact VIA Rail Special Needs Services (888-842-7245 or 800-268-9503/TDD; www.viarail.ca). For information about bus travel, contact

BC Ferries

Greyhound Canada (800-397-7870/TDD; www.greyhound.ca). Additional information is available from the BC Office for Disability Issues (250-356-5991 or 250-387-3114/TDD); or from the We're Accessible Quarterly (to request a copy, call 604-576-5075).

ACCOMMODATIONS

For a selection of places to stay overnight, see Hotels at the back of the guide.

Reservations Services

Tourism Vancouver – 604-683-2000; www.tourismvancouver.com.
Tourism BC – 250-387-1642 or 800-663-6000; www.hellobc.com.
British Columbia Bed & Breakfast Innkeepers Guild – www.bcsbestbnbs.com.
BBCanada – www.bbcanada.com

Major hotel and motel chains have locations in Vancouver:
- **Best Western** – 800-780-7234 www.bestwestern.com.
- **Choice Hotels** – 877-424-6423 www.choicehotels.com.
- **Days Inn** – 800-225-3297 www.daysinn.com.
- **Delta Hotels** – 888-890-3222 www.deltahotels.com.
- **Fairmont** – 800-257-7544 www.fairmont.com.
- **Four Seasons** – 800-HIL-TONS www.fourseasons.com.
- **Hilton** – 800-221-2424 www.hilton.com.
- **Holiday Inn** – 877-660-8550 www.holidayinn.com.
- **Marriott** – 888-236-2427 www.marriott.com.
- **Radisson Inn** – 800-967-9033 www.radisson.com.
- **Ramada Inn** – 800-854-9517 www.ramada.com.

- **Sheraton** – 800-325-3535 www.starwoodhotels.com/sheraton.
- **Westin** – 800-937-8461 www.starwoodhotels.com/westin.

Campgrounds
BC Parks: 800-689-9025; www.env.gov.bc.ca/bcparks

Hostels
There are three large hostels in Vancouver, two downtown and one at Jericho Beach (*see Hotels*). Many other destinations in BC have hostels; contact Hostelling International-Canada (800-663-5777 or www.hihostels.ca) for other hostels in the province.

COMMUNICATIONS

To call long distance within Canada and to the US from landline phones, dial 1+ **area code** + number. For overseas calls, refer to the country codes in most telephone directories, or dial "0" for operator assistance. Many operators in Canada speak English and French. Collect calls and credit card calls can be made from public pay phones, which are becoming ever more uncommon.

For local directory assistance, check the white pages of the phone directory or dial 411 (fee may apply); outside the local area code, dial 1+ area code + 555-1212. Telephone numbers that start with **800, 866, 877** or **888** are toll-free (no charge) to North American phone service customers, though some European phones cannot utilize these toll-free numbers. A local call costs 50 cents. Be aware that many hotels place a surcharge on all calls.

PRACTICAL INFORMATION

Area Codes

Throughout British Columbia, you must dial the **area code** plus the seven-digit number to make a local phone call. Before you leave, check with your home carrier to ensure your **cell phone** will operate in Canada. Area codes for Vancouver and the Lower Mainland, including Whistler are 604 and 778.
Rest of British Columbia, including Victoria and Vancouver Island: 250 and 778.

Cell/Mobile Phones

Cell (mobile) phone coverage is widespread in and around British Columbia's cities, towns and popular tourist attractions but remains sketchy or nonexistent in remote areas of the province. Coverage varies with different carriers, but most phones have full service in cities and towns. Some cell phones whose providers cover most of North America do not require the initial '1' for long distance; users simply dial the applicable 10-digit number to reach phones anywhere in Canada and the US.

Emergency Numbers

911 service, operated through municipalities, is extensive in British Columbia, and can be accessed from cell phones; if for some reason 911 doesn't work, dial "0" for the operator and ask for the police.

Internet Access

High-speed Internet service (Wi-Fi) is available in virtually all hotels in Vancouver, Whistler and on Vancouver Island, as well as in many restaurants and coffee shops. Some visitor centres might provide Internet access.

BASIC INFORMATION
Discounts

Prices in this guide are shown for a single adult only, unless otherwise stated. Discounts may be available for the following:
Senior Citizens – Many attractions, hotels, restaurants, entertainment venues and public transportation systems offer discounts to visitors age 62 or older (proof of age may be required). Canada's national parks usually offer discount fees for seniors.

Important Phone Numbers	
Emergency (police, ambulance, fire department, 24hrs)	✆**911**
Police (non-emergency)	✆604-717-3535
Crime Stoppers	✆800-222-8477
24-hour Pharmacy Shoppers Drug Mart, 1125 Davie Street	✆604-669-2424
Weather	✆604-664-9010
Road Conditions	✆604-660-9770 ✆800-550-4997
Canadian Automobile Association	✆604-293-2222

Measurement Equivalents									
Degrees Fahrenheit	95°	86°	77°	68°	59°	50°	41°	32°	23°	14°
Degrees Celsius	35°	30°	25°	20°	15°	10°	5°	0°	-5°	-10°

1 inch = 2.54 centimeters (cm)
1 mile = 1.6 kilometers (km)
1 quart = 0.94 liters
1 foot = 30.48 centimeters (cm)

1 ounce = 28 grams (gm)
1 pound = 0.45 kilograms (kg)
1 gallon = 3.78 litres

For more information, contact the Canadian Association for the 50 Plus (www.50plus.com) or the Canadian Association of Retired Persons (888-363-2279; www.carp.ca). Visiting seniors should feel free to ask specific businesses if a discount is available. **Students** – Discounted prices might be available for students with proof of student status. Be sure to ask.

Electricity
Voltage in Canada is 120 volts AC, 60 Hz. Foreign-made appliances may need AC adapters (available at specialty travel and electronics stores) and North American two-prong, flat-blade plugs.

Mail/Post
Post offices across Canada are generally open Monday to Friday 8am–5:30pm; extended hours are available in some locations. Sample rates for first-class mail (letter or postcard; up to 30 grams): within Canada 59 cents; to the US $1.03; international mail $1.75. Note that rates typically rise every year, in January. **"P" stamps** do not show a value and can be used indefinitely once they are purchased. Mail service for all but local deliveries is by air. For information regarding postal codes or locations of facilities, visit www.canadapost.ca.

Metric System
Canada has adopted the International System of weights and measures. Weather **temperatures** are given in Celsius (°C), milk, other fluids and wine are sold by millilitres and litres, and grocery items are measured in grams. All distances and **speed limits** are posted in kilometres (to obtain the approximate equivalent in miles, multiply by 0.6). *See chart above.*

Money
Canadian Currency – Canada's currency is based on the **decimal system** (100 cents to the dollar). Bills are issued in $5, $10, $20, $50, $100 and $500 denominations; coins are minted in 5 cents, 10 cents, 25 cents, $1 and $2. (Effective November 2012, the penny is no longer being produced.) The Canadian dollar fluctuates with international exchange rates, usually within 10 percent of the value of the US dollar. All prices shown in this guide are in Canadian dollars unless otherwise specified.
Credit/Debit Cards – You don't need to carry much cash while visiting Canada: ATM machines are widely available, and most merchants accept debit or credit cards. Self-serve gas stations, parking lots and even grocery store check-outs are common vendors

where credit and debit cards are accepted. Do carry a few "loonies" or "toonies" (the $1 and $2 coins) for parking meters, tips and snacks. Most public telephones accept calling cards at no charge, but local calls cost 50 cents (two quarters). To report a lost or stolen credit card: American Express (800-668-2639); Diners Club (866-890-9552); MasterCard (800-307-7309); or Visa (800-336-8472).

Currency Exchange – Exchange money at banks for a favourable **exchange rate**. The most favourable rate may be through credit card companies. Visitors can exchange currency at downtown banks as well as at Vancouver International Airport. Most banks charge a percentage fee for this transaction. Private exchange companies generally charge higher fees. Airports and visitor centres in large cities may have exchange outlets, as do some hotels.

Travellers' Cheques – Some banks, stores, restaurants and hotels accept travellers' cheques with photo identification. However, many merchants today are reluctant to accept traveller's cheques. In addition, Canadian bank systems have converted to the chip-and-pin credit cards used in Europe, but US-style magnetic-stripe cards are still usable at many self-serve pay-points. US travellers are best advised to buy gas at stations with registers manned by clerks who can process a signature purchase, as a precaution.

Opening Hours

Business hours in British Columbia are, for the most part, Monday to Friday 10am–5pm. In general, retail stores are open Monday to Friday 9am–6pm (until 9pm Thursday and Friday), Saturday 9am–5pm, with Sunday hours noon–5pm. In most cities, shops are usually open on Sunday afternoon; many small convenience stores in gas stations may be open much longer hours.

Banking institutions are generally open Monday to Friday 9am–5pm; some bank branches are open on Saturday morning, and some offer extended evening hours.

Smoking

British Columbia has one of the toughest anti-smoking laws in North America. Smoking is banned in all public spaces, including restaurants, bars and private clubs, building lobbies and any other enclosed space where people gather. There may be designated smoking rooms in hospitals and health institutions, but otherwise the only public place you can light up is outdoors, and not near (within 3 metres) a door, windows or air intake.

Smoking has been banned from aircraft, buses, trains and most offices for some time. Visitors may still smoke in their own hotel rooms; many hotels continue to have smoking floors.

Spectator Sports

Vancouver is a great place to be a spectator at sporting events. The city's major professional sports teams include:

- **Football/BC Lions (Canadian Football League)**
  late June–November
  BC Place
  604-589-7627
  www.bclions.com

Vancouver Canadians baseball game
©Vancouver Canadians

- **Hockey/Vancouver Canucks**
  (National Hockey League)
  October–June
  Rogers Arena
  604-899-7000
  http://canucks.nhl.com
- **Baseball/**
  Vancouver Canadians
  (Northwest League of
  Professional Baseball)
  April–September
  Nat Bailey Stadium
  604-872-5232
  www.canadiansbaseball.com

Taxes

Prices displayed in Canada do
not include sales tax.

Vancouver Taxes – Effective
April 1, 2013, the former HST
(Harmonized Sales Tax) will be
returned to a split federal and
provincial sales tax, distinct from
other provinces in Canada. In
British Columbia, the federal
portion (Goods and Services Tax
or GST) is 5 percent; the Provincial
Sales Tax (PST) is 7 percent. There
is a 10 percent lodging tax in
Vancouver.

Time Zone

Vancouver is located in the Pacific
Standard Time zone (PST), eight
hours behind Greenwich Mean
Time and three hours behind
New York City.

Tipping

It is customary to give a small gift
of money—a tip—for services
rendered to the following service
providers: waiters (15–20 percent
of bill), porters ($1 per bag),
chambermaids ($1 per day) and
taxi drivers (15 percent of fare).

PORT OF CALL: VANCOUVER

Canada's largest port on its western coast, Vancouver is home to dozens of cruise lines that tour the coast south and north of the city, as well as points on Vancouver Island such as Victoria and Nanaimo.

A Top Destination

Vancouver is a destination for cruise ships as well as a popular port of call for multi-stop cruises that sail the Pacific Northwest and the South Pacific. While Vancouver itself is a huge draw for cruise-ship tourism, it is perhaps best known as being the embarking point for ships traveling to **Alaska**. Most major cruise lines offer Alaska cruises from Vancouver; some include Vancouver in their ports of call for cruises from San Francisco, and points north.

The ideal Vancouver-based cruise offers the best of the two worlds that the city straddles: staggeringly beautiful natural scenery and the vibrancy of the world-class city. A combination of coastal cruising and land excursions to spots such as

Whistler, **Fraser Valley** wineries, **Granville Island**, North Vancouver and **Victoria** is a perfect blend. There are, of course, locally operated **small-cruise companies** that take guests on runs through English Bay and Burrard Inlet, among other popular spots within the city and surrounds, but don't go out to sea. Some offer dinner cruises and others daytime tours. Others still can be rented for dedicated private parties.

Due to weather restrictions, cruises heading north through the **Inside Passage** and up to Alaska operate from May to September. Many of Alaska's glaciers will still be ice-packed in summer, so this is an ideal time to enjoy the luxury of the cruise while marvelling at inlets and fjords and humpback whales.

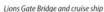
Lions Gate Bridge and cruise ship

Cruises Lines

A number of cruise lines serve the port of Vancouver, Vancouver Island and Victoria. Opposite is a selection of the major lines calling in the area.

Celebrity Cruises

www.celebritycruises.com or 1-800-647-2251.

Celebrity offers primarily cruises that depart Vancouver and make the Alaskan coast run, with stops at the **Prince William Sound** glaciers, Brooks Falls at Katmai National Park and **Juneau**, with views of Mount McKinley (weather permitting). This company also sails the more southerly Pacific coastline with Wine Cruises from San Francisco to Vancouver, including stops at Victoria and Nanaimo in British Columbia, and Seattle in Washington State.

Holland America Line

www.hollandamerica.com or 1-877-932-4259.

Holland America delivers shoreline cruises to explore the immediate areas around Vancouver, including the Capilano Suspension Bridge, Chinatown, Gastown and Stanley Park, and **Butchart Gardens** on Vancouver Island. Vancouver is a destination vacation for this cruise line, as well as presenting Vancouver as a port of call on their multi-port packages.

They offer spectacular 24- and 58-day Pacific cruises that stop at Vancouver, as well as exotic locales like Sydney, Australia, Hawaii, Pogo Pogo, Fiji and New Caledonia. A relaxing long weekend could comprise a three-day cruise that stops at Vancouver, Astoria (Oregon) and San Francisco.

Norwegian Cruise Line

www.ncl.com or 1-866-234-7350.

Norwegian endeavours to give travellers a lot in a compact period, with 7-day cruises that include stops at San Francisco, Los Angeles, Vancouver, Victoria, Nanaimo, and Astoria. They also provide week-long cruises from Vancouver to Alaska. One of the most reasonably priced of the major carriers, especially if travellers book early.

Oceania Cruises

www.oceaniacruises.com or 1-800-531-5619.

A slightly smaller organization that pays particular attention to upscale details, Oceania Cruises start sailing from Vancouver to Alaska and back in mid-May; booking well in advance can net as much as a 50 percent discount and optimum luxury while you visit and see the **Inside Passage**, Ketchikan, Juneau, Sitka and Wrangell, with an awe-inspiring pause at Tracy Arm Fjord and Sawyer Glacier.

Princess Cruises

www.princess.com or 1-800-774-6237.

One of the world's favourite cruise lines, Princess has been running the **Vancouver-to-Alaska** route for about four decades and knows what travellers want most. With extended stay options, visitors can spend more or less time in Vancouver as they choose, and can enjoy **add-on excursions** to highlights such as Stanley Park, Robson Street and Granville Island. Most of the Alaska-bound cruises include a visit to Victoria, and focus on the star attractions of Alaska: fjords, glaciers and whales.

PACIFIC RIM PARADISE

Sparkling Vancouver is truly a city of the world. Poised on North America's Pacific Rim—and at the forefront of urban life—this cosmopolitan city boasts a spectacular natural setting, a diverse economy, high marks from both residents and visitors, and a level of cultural diversity matched by few other metropolitan areas.

It's all about lifestyle here. Vancouver has it all: a mild climate, fabulous restaurants, world-class hotels, great cultural attractions, recreational opportunities and stunning scenery. It's no wonder that Vancouver has always been rated highly among hundreds of competitors as the the **"most liveable city"** in the world," ranking third in 2012.

The place now called Vancouver was once just large, lofty trees surrounded by shellfish-laden beaches and salmon-rich waters, and populated by the **First Nations peoples**. Although the waters of British Columbia (BC) were first explored by Spanish seafarers, it was British Royal Navy officer Captain **George Vancouver** who charted the area for Britain in 1793. The first European settlers, trappers and traders established posts for the **Hudson's Bay Company** in the early 1800s. In 1858 the discovery of gold in the BC interior brought global attention to the region, but the real wealth of the coast turned out to be **timber**.

In 1863 the first sawmill was built on Burrard Inlet, and as the towering old-growth Douglas firs and western red cedars were felled, development sprang up in the clearings. European, Asian and American immigrants flocked to BC in the latter half of the 19C to work in the timber and fishing industries. When the **Canadian Pacific Railway** chose Burrard Inlet as the terminus for its transcontinental rail line in 1885, Vancouver's future was assured. Today Vancouver thrives as Canada's Pacific hub, the largest port in the country—trade in BC as

Downtown Vancouver

INTRODUCTION

a whole supports approximately 20 percent of area jobs. **Tourism** has assumed huge significance, with nearly 9 million visitors a year to Vancouver.

The city hosts the annual Vancouver International Film Festival, held in the early fall since 1982. The **film industry** spends more than $1.2 billion annually in and around the city. Filmmakers like the fact that BC's diverse landscape means that somewhere within a few hours of Vancouver is a setting that can substitute for almost any place in the world; the city's famously temperate climate assures virtually nonstop production. That moderate *terroir* also enables BC growers to produce a vast array of fruits, vegetables, herbs and wines that Vancouver chefs utilize, blending continental and Asian influences with Pacific seafood, to create a distinctive regional fusion fare known as **West Coast cuisine**.

For the visitor, Vancouver is a remarkably user-friendly city. Although there are no freeways, travel from the airport to downtown takes less than a half-hour. Once you're downtown, the vast majority of attractions are

West Hastings Street, about 1900

©Philip Timms/Vancouver Public Library Historical Photos

within **walking distance**—Stanley Park, the Art Gallery, Canada Place, Gastown, Chinatown, Yaletown. Canadians are uniformly helpful and friendly, and the currency **exchange rate** has traditionally favoured those spending American dollars, British pounds and euros, but in recent years has mostly been on par with the US dollar. On top of all that, everywhere you look is **spectacular scenery**: glistening blue water, majestic forests, and towering snowcapped mountains.

The proximity of these landscapes encourages skiing, golf, hiking, boating and other outdoor recreation for many adventurous residents and visitors alike.

PACIFIC RIM PARADISE

35

NEIGHBOURHOODS

Take some time to get to know Vancouver's distinctive neighbourhoods. The vibrant West End is one of the densest residential districts in North America, and home to Vancouver's gay and lesbian community. Kitsilano is a slightly gentrified former hippie haven that is now a wonderful place for families to live and work. Dazzling and energetic, hip Yaletown borders a massive urban development, Concord Place, which has transfigured what was left of the Expo '86 grounds. Chinatown is one of the best areas for a morning stroll in any city.

CHINATOWN★★

Bounded by Keefer, Abbott and Hastings Sts. and Gore Ave. www.virtualvancouver.com/chinatown.html.

Though Vancouver's Chinatown is small by North American neighbourhood standards, it is big by Chinatown measurements—the **third-largest**, exceeded only by Chinatowns in New York and San Francisco. It dates back almost 150 years, to the days when Chinese laborers were brought across the Pacific Ocean to build the Canadian railroads and wagon roads. Its continuing vitality reflects the mid-1990s exodus from Hong Kong to Canada, as well as Canada's history of welcoming immigrants. To this day, more than half the district's residents list Mandarin or Cantonese as their native language.

It's best to explore Chinatown on foot, so you can take in the sights, sounds, smells and tastes of the dynamic Asian cultural mix; start at Pender and Carrall streets, head east three blocks to Gore, then south a block and back west on Keefer Street. Along the way, the exotic world of **Asian life** flavours every step. Numerous food stalls offer dozens of different Pacific

Roof detail, Chinatown

©AIBC

Touring Tip

Though Chinatown itself is perfectly safe during the day, the stretch of **Hastings Street** west of the district is an area plagued by drug trafficking, and it's not advisable to walk through it at any time, day or night. To walk to Chinatown from downtown, it's best to take **Pender Street.** The intersection of Main and Hastings streets, in front of the old Carnegie Library, suffers the same problem—tread warily.

Jade Water Pavilion, Dr. Sun Yat-Sen Classical Chinese Garden

seafood varieties, and large tanks of crab and lobster. Other stalls overflow with everything from dried fish (used for flavouring) to glistening honey-glazed roast quail—which makes a great mid-morning snack. Keep your eyes peeled for jackfruit, an enormous tropical fruit bigger than a watermelon.

The Best of Chinatown
Dr. Sun Yat-Sen Classical Chinese Garden★

578 Carrall St. at Keefer St.
See also Parks and Gardens.

This classical Chinese garden is the district's visitor highlight, but the smaller, less developed **meditation garden** adjacent to it *(toward Quebec St.)* is also lovely in its own right, and there's no admission charge. Both gardens honour the father of modern China, Sun Yat-Sen (1866–1925).

Chinese Benevolent Association

[A] refer to map on inside front cover. 108 E. Pender St.

The association's home (1909) is a lavishly painted example of a tong headquarters—**tongs** being community support associations, not the pseudo-gangs as often supposed.

Chinatown Classics

Tea is more than simply a beverage to the Chinese, and at **Ten Lee Hong Tea & Ginseng** (*500 Main St.; 604-689-7598*) you can experience a formal tea ceremony and investigate the dozens of medicinal uses for ginseng—which would truly be a miracle substance if it accomplished everything its adherents claimed it did. Fans of Chinese cooking won't want to miss **Ming Wo** (*23 E. Pender St.; 604-683-7268; www.mingwo.com*), a small warehouse stacked floor-to-ceiling with cookware, including the greatest variety of woks you're ever likely to see. Established in 1917, the store now has four downtown locations, and one each in North Vancouver, Richmond and Burnaby.

NEIGHBOURHOODS

Chinese Cultural Centre Museum & Archives

555 Columbia St. 604-658-8880. www.cccvan.com. Open Tue–Sun 11am–5pm.

Adjacent to the Sun Yat-Sen garden, the cultural centre was founded in 1973 to foster understanding of the Chinese people and to promote Chinese culture and art. It accomplishes these goals by hosting special events, celebrations and language classes, as well as changing art exhibits.

The centre also houses an evocative **museum** describing the painful experience of Chinese-Canadians in their new homeland and their forced imprisonment during World War II. Upstairs, you'll learn about the impressive record of Chinese-Canadians who served in the country's military.

Chinese Freemasons Building

[B] refer to map on inside front cover. 5 W. Pender St., northwest corner of Pender and Carrall Sts.

It is rumored that Sun Yat-Sen secretly lived in this 1907 structure when he came to Vancouver in the early 20C. Here he plotted with the Cheekungton, a powerful Chinese secret society, to overthrow the Manchu government in China.

Sam Kee Building

[C] refer to map on inside front cover. 8 W. Pender St., southwest corner of Pender & Carrall Sts.

At 1.8m/6ft wide, this two-storey building claims to be the world's narrowest office building. A property-line dispute forced the narrow design of the structure. It now houses an insurance agency, and yes, employees work therein.

Chinatown Cuisine: Dim Sum

One of the many translations of this Mandarin term is "little treats"—and each serving is indeed small, and a treat. But a meal composed of a half-dozen dim sum baskets is anything but modest—baked, fried or steamed pastries, buns, cakes and dumplings are always filling and intensely flavoured. Common "packaging" materials include wheat, rice and taro flour; some dim sum arrive wrapped in banana leaves; some have no wrapping at all, like the chicken feet that fascinate—and repel—most Westerners. Fillings include shrimp, oysters, fish, squid and other seafood; pork and chicken; bean pastes and tofu; custards and fruit preparations.

Chefs arrive at the crack of dawn at dim sum restaurants to prepare the day's selection of up to 50 types of morsels; midday diners start arriving just before noon, and the "dim sum ladies" begin trundling up and down the aisles, offering customers the chance to peek at what's in the basket or on the platter. It's best to go with friends and sample many different kinds—don't be afraid to be adventurous. Unless you're fluent in Mandarin or Cantonese, you may not always know exactly what's in each item, but there's fun in the mystery. Gourmands can take heart in the fact that there are estimated to be more than 500 kinds of dim sum, with new ones being created all the time.

Filming Stargate Atlantis

Set Pieces

Though *The X-Files* brought Vancouver new prominence, the city has long been a film industry magnet—and it remains so, with more than $1 billion in TV and film production a year in BC. There is literally never a day that a production isn't shooting somewhere in or around Vancouver—Stanley Park, the Art Gallery grounds, Gastown and Yaletown are common settings. You are quite likely to encounter a film shoot by chance, but you can refine the process considerably by contacting the **BC Film Commission** for a list of current productions and locations (*BC Film Commission, 201-865 Hornby St.; 604-660-2732; www.bcfilmcommission.com*).

Please bear in mind that, among other things, the industry likes Vancouver because city residents believe in practicing simple courtesy with stars: it's fine to watch them, but not to invade their privacy.

Floata Seafood Restaurant

180 Keefer St. 604-602-0368.
www.floata.com.

With headquarters in Hong Kong, the largest Chinese restaurant in Canada can seat 1,000 (yes, one thousand) people. Almost every table will be filled on a busy day; don't arrive late. Specialties include Peking duck, which is barbecued on-site.

WEST END★

Bounded by Thurlow St., False Creek and English Bay, Stanley Park and Georgia St.

With high-rise apartments packed cheek-to-jowl along tree-lined streets, the West End is what Vancouver officials claim is the highest-density residential area in North America. The heart of the neighbourhood is **Denman Street,** a European-style artery lined with small shops, cafes and bistros. Here, fruit and vegetable vendors offer fresh produce from all climes and culinary persuasions, and local independent coffee houses compete with larger national chains like the ubiquitous Canadian coffee shop, Tim Hortons, and Starbucks.

Touring Tip

Take a gelati break morning, noon or night: be sure to stop in at **Milano Coffee & Gelato** (*849 Denman St.; 604-681-1500*) to sample the dozens of Italian-style gelati and ices.

The West End was the first "suburban" residential development in the young city's life—city fathers prevailed on Cornelius van Horne, the ultra-powerful nabob of the Canadian Pacific Railway, to use his influence in Ottawa to back Vancouver's plea for title to a military reserve— now **Stanley Park**. The park made the new West End housing development considerably more attractive. The neighbourhood's transition to high-rise apartments occurred largely in the period between World War II and 1960.

English Bay Beach★★

Beach Ave. and Denman St.

If you're in Vancouver in the winter, spring or fall months, you may wonder why the beach here looks so neatly tended, the sand raked and logs lined up back from the water. Do people really swim here? Yes, they do. In July, August and early September, English Bay's shallow water warms sufficiently to welcome all but the wimpiest souls. By noon on sunny days, assorted families and sunbathers, with their towels and picnic baskets, will be spread out by every log. Kayakers paddle by; kids splash in the shallows; and every once in a while, when the wake from a container ship reaches shore, intrepid body surfers hop on a break for a short ride. When you're lying on the beach with the palm gardens (*see Parks and Gardens*) behind you, it's not easy to believe you're in the homeland of ice hockey.

◆ **English Bay Bathhouse** offers showers and a place to change; it rents kayaks and sailboards, as well.

West End Markets

Capers, at 1675 Robson Street, is the city's leading natural-foods outlet, and a great place to get a sandwich for lunch (*604-687-5288*); there is also a location at 2285 4th Ave. W., in Kitsilano. The **Robson Public Market** (*1610 Robson St.*) is an indoor aggregation of butchers, bakers, delis and produce vendors (no candlestick-makers) who sell everything from North European sausages to East Asian rice dishes. Cuisines available to passersby range from fiery Korean at **Madangcoul** (*847 Denman St.; 604-688-3585*) to delectable Spanish at **Tapastree** (*1829 Robson St.; 604-606-4680; www. tapastree.ca*).

Coffee Capital

You'll notice something interesting about the intersection of Robson and Thurlow streets. On the southwest corner is a Starbucks (often visited by motorcycle riders). On the northeast corner is, yes, another Starbucks. Both stores do a thriving business. Vancouverites

West End Farmers' Market

©City of Vancouver

cede the title of most-coffee-crazed city to no one!

Roedde House Museum

1415 Barclay St. See Historic Sites.

YALETOWN★

Bounded by Davie, Homer, Nelson and Cambie Sts., and Pacific Blvd.

Yaletown isn't the only former **warehouse district** given new life by redevelopment, but it's certainly one of the best-known and the most dynamic. What was, just 20 or so years ago, a decaying area dedicated to the business of produce shipping has been transformed into a bustling commercial district filled with hip restaurants, galleries and shops. Long before it was a warehouse district, Yaletown was the edge of a tidal flatland. The curving brick wall in the tiny park at Mainland and Davie streets marks the shoreline of two centuries ago, before dredging and filling converted much of **False Creek** to dry land. That area was also the site of the Expo '86 fairgrounds, which have recently been converted into a massive housing complex called **Concord Pacific Place**.
It all happens along two blocks of Hamilton and Mainland streets (between Nelson & Davie Sts.). Perched above these two streets, behind the loading docks that once served delivery trucks—now turned into patios and a broad promenade—are some of the city's glitziest restaurants, toniest shops and finest salons. The scene on a pleasant evening, when young

---

Roundhouse Community Arts & Recreation Centre

181 Roundhouse Mews, in the Concord Pacific Place development.
604-713-1800; www.roundhouse.ca.

Once upon a time Canadian Pacific engineers used the huge turntable here to juggle locomotives and railcars. The railroad is long gone, but the turntable forms the centrepiece of the courtyard for an intriguing neighbourhood centre. Outside, a massive retired locomotive thrills kids and rail fans, while the gallery space inside features temporary shows by local artists and craftspeople. It's a worthy reminder of this now chic neighbourhood's gritty past.

©City of Vancouver

NEIGHBOURHOODS

office workers flock to the area, rivals that of Greenwich Village or Soho in New York City.

Yaletown Sampler

Here are some "musts" among Yaletown's many restaurants and shops:

◆ **Barbara Jo's Books to Cooks** – 1740 West 2nd Ave. 604-688-6755. www.bookstocooks.com.

◆ **Blue Water Cafe + Raw Bar** – 1095 Hamilton St. 604-688-8078. www.bluewatercafe.net.

◆ **Chintz & Company** – 950 Homer St. 604-689-2022. www.chintz.com.

◆ **Cioppino's Mediterranean Grill** – 1133 Hamilton St. 604-688-7466. www.cioppinosyaletown.com.

◆ **Vancouver Cigar Company** – 1093 Hamilton St. 604-685-0445. www.vancouvercigar.com.

KITSILANO

Bounded by Burrard St., W. 12th Ave., MacDonald St. and False Creek/English Bay.

"I've got a nice little place in Kits," is the way that thousands of Vancouverites happily explain their residences—and thousands more wish they could. Indeed, thriving, progressive Kitsilano enjoys the best reputation among all Vancouver's residential districts. From 1966 and into the '70s, peace signs were prominent front-door insignias, a VW van was parked on almost every block, and a protest of some sort was the subject of constant telephone-pole posters. Nearby **Vanier Park** witnessed any number of be-ins and demonstrations. When the

---

Quintessential Kitsilano

Sophie's Cosmic Cafe

2095 West 4th Ave. 604-732-6810. www.sophiescosmiccafe.com.

With its "garage sale" decor, and a menu that ranges from waffles to falafel to veggie burgers and quesadillas, Sophie's is an institution that has withstood the many tides of change running through Kitsilano.

Since it opened in the 1940s, the cafe has specialized in huge breakfast plates, bowls of rich oyster stew, and deep-dish apple pie that towers seven inches high.

Banyen Books & Sound

3608 W. 4th Ave. 604-732-7912. www.banyen.com. Here you'll find a copy of seemingly every self-help book ever written, as well as a CD inventory that includes flute music from every continent. Founded in the early 1970s, Banyen devotes itself to

Banyen Books & Sound

Banyen Books & Sound

personal growth in a thoroughly ecumenical fashion—volumes on everything from Buddhist to Zoroastrian thought, and music ranging from Gregorian chants to Paul Winter. Banyen does a thriving business shipping its books and CDs throughout North America.

Monster Homes

Though Shaughnessy itself remains much as it was 75 years ago, the districts on either side of Granville and Oak, and to the south toward the airport, experienced a phenomenon in the mid-1990s whose result is conspicuous today. Huge, newly built, château-like houses crowd next to each other on small lots that once held much smaller residences. These "monster homes," as long-time Vancouverites call them, were built by wealthy immigrants from Hong Kong who came to Canada to avoid the Chinese takeover of the former British colony in 1997. Taking advantage of their Commonwealth passports, and cashing in their Asian fortunes, the new settlers purchased old houses, tore down the small buildings, and replaced them with the biggest homes building codes would allow. Ironically, many of those who fled to Vancouver before 1997 have now returned to Hong Kong.

entire city was virtually shut down by antiwar protests in March and April 1967, Kitsilano was the heart of the action. In the 21C, the neighbourhood still leans heavily leftward; some of those same activists are now long-term residents who have raised their families here.

Bordering Vanier Park along the English Bay shore, Kitsilano is paradise for those who love the outdoors. Neighbourhood amenities include Kitsilano Beach, Vancouver's largest outdoor pool (a mix of fresh and salt water), sand volleyball courts, a walking-biking-in-line skating path, and easy access to downtown—a 20minute walk across the **Burrard Bridge**.

Craftsman-style Gems

You'll find some of Canada's best examples of Craftsman-style residential architecture in serene Kitsilano. The biggest and best ones are near **Vanier Park** (*between Chestnut and Arbutus Sts., north of Cornwall St.*).

SHAUGHNESSY

Bounded by Granville St., W.12th Ave., Oak St.and W. 33rd Ave.

This is Vancouver's original **mansion district**, a sublime hill where the city's first tycoons (such as timber baron H.R. MacMillan) who made their fortunes in the lumber, rail and trade industries, built stone and timber mansions in the early 20C. Curving streets (the city's first) wind past **palatial homes** of granite and fir, with broad lawns, semicircular drives, perfectly trimmed hedges and spreading oaks and maples. It looks like the baronial English neighbourhood it was intended to be when it was developed by the Canadian Pacific Railway in 1907. Although this isn't the priciest real estate in the Vancouver area any more (that title goes to the West Vancouver waterfront), a drive along Shaughnessy's quiet streets still produces its share of "oohs" and "ahhs." Descendants of the original residents now share their neighbourhood with Hollywood stars who rent homes here during film shoots.

LANDMARKS

You'll recognize Vancouver's cityscape by the blue-glass and brushed-metal style of the buildings that line the waterfronts along False Creek and Coal Harbour. Most of the city's landmarks date from the 20C, as Vancouver was founded in 1886, but a ferocious fire destroyed much of it shortly after it was incorporated. Whereas Gastown *(see Historic Sites)* preserves the city's pre-1900 buildings, the finest examples of contemporary architectural design occupy downtown along a one-mile loop that makes an easy walk. So put on your sneakers and sunglasses—the glare off the glass buildings on a sunny day can be fierce—and look at the landmarks that define this international city.

LANDMARK BUILDINGS

Canada Place★★

999 Canada Place Way, at the foot of Howe St. 604-775-7200. www.canadaplace.ca. Promenade open 24hrs daily. IMAX shows daily noon–10pm; $11.50.

You can't help but notice the white "ship" moored in **Burrard Inlet**. After almost a quarter-century, it has become an icon of Vancouver. The graceful canvas "sails" of Canada Place lift 70m/230ft above the water below.

Designed by Zeidler Partnership Architects, headed by Eberhard

Zeidler, Canada Place was opened in 1986. Built by the federal government for Expo '86, the structure acted as Canada's pavilion during the fair. For the 2010 Olympics, it served double duty as the press centre.

Aside from their obvious reference to the city's lifelong connection to maritime affairs, the **roof peaks,** held aloft by central pillars, make room for large open areas within the city's convention centre underneath. With massive cruise ships docked alongside, the whole structure is eminently practical, no matter how fanciful it appears.

Head up to the second-level **promenade** for wonderful

Promenade at Canada Place

canadaplace.ca

views★★ of the harbour, Stanley Park and the North Shore mountains. An **IMAX theatre** housed within shows big-screen films, whose topics range from NASCAR auto racing to Everest exploration. The top-notch **Pan Pacific Hotel** *(see Hotels)* occupies the southwest corner of the building, next to the Vancouver World Trade Centre. A **pedestrian path** departs from the southwest corner to Stanley Park, which is about a 10-minute walk away.

Library Square★★

350 W. Georgia St. 604-331-3603. www.vpl.Vancouver.bc.ca. Open Mon–Thu 10am–9pm, Fri–Sat 10am–6pm, Sun noon–5pm.

Is it a grandiose imitation of ancient architecture—or a memorable addition to the Vancouver landscape? Hardly anyone is neutral about this colourful design by famed Canadian architect Moshe Safdie. Safdie denies the building's similarities to the **Roman Colosseum**—but the resemblance is obvious to virtually everyone else. Made of brown pre-cast concrete, the complex opened in 1995, and houses the main Public Library, government offices, retail shops and a splendid **outdoor plaza** that's great for 🚶 **people-watching** on sunny days. Nay-sayers who find the whole thing too much should glance across the street, at the Vancouver Post Office *(on the north side of Georgia St.)*. **Library Lowdown** – The seven-level Public Library is one of the largest anywhere, with 1.2 million items, a large children's library, extensive audio-visual and electronic materials sections, and numerous nooks and crannies that are specifically designed to provide private reading spots. **Sky bridges** that span the seven-storey **atrium** are guaranteed to wrinkle the brows of anyone with acrophobia. The ground floor holds coffee shops, cafes and small retailers.

BC Place Stadium★

777 Pacific Blvd. 604-669-2300. www.bcplacestadium.com.

Though some have derided its appearance as a puff pastry left out too long, this fabric-dome-roofed structure has

©Vancouver Public Library

Library Square

45

Cathedral Place

[D] refers to map on the inside front cover. 925 W. Georgia St. at Hornby St.

This 1990 office tower was expressly designed to blend with its historic companions—the copper roof and gargoyles mimic the **Hotel Vancouver** across Georgia Street, and the Art Deco touches reflect the 1920s building it replaced. Ground-floor stonework, meanwhile, corresponds to **Christ Church Cathedral** to the west.

served its role admirably since 1983. More recently it was an essential element of the 2010 Winter Olympics for opening and closing ceremonies, and medal presentations. (Olympic bid organizers pointed out that using BC Place would alleviate fears of rain-drenched ceremonies at a snow-sports extravaganza.) Now sporting a new cable-supported **retractable roof**, said to be the largest roof of its kind on earth, the 55,000-seat stadium is homefield for the **BC Lions** Canadian Football League team, and a venue for rock and pop concerts, car and home shows and the like.

BC Sports Hall of Fame and Museum★

In BC Place. See For Kids.

Christ Church Cathedral★

690 Burrard St. at Georgia St. 604-682-3848. www.cathedral vancouver.bc.ca. Open before and after worship services, for concerts, and for tours by appointment.

Outside, solid sandstone. Inside, massive hewn timbers bracing the roof. Though this is the seat of the Anglican diocese of Vancouver (it became a cathedral in 1929), it was built in 1889 to remind its members of parish churches back

in Britain. Now the edifice is the **oldest church** in the city, from a time when the area was residential. Its steep, **gabled roof**, arched windows and huge stained-glass windows are architectural treasures.

The church is frequently the site of concerts and other performances, both religious and secular. Plans to demolish the cathedral and sell the land for an office tower aroused a huge controversy in the late 1970s. In the end, the Episcopal diocese sold the density rights to the land to the developers of Cathedral Place just north *(see sidebar)*, allowing that building to rise taller, and gaining money for renovation of the church.

Harbour Centre Tower★

555 W. Hastings St.

Even after a quarter-century, this ungainly 167.5m/550ft landmark on West Hastings Street is, at 45 storeys high, Vancouver's second-tallest building, after the 62-storey Living Shangri-La was erected in 2008.

The circular pod atop the tower houses a **viewing platform** and restaurant *(see For Fun)*; you can access it via a glass-walled elevator. The late astronaut Neil Armstrong officially opened the building in August 1977, leaving behind—you guessed it—a footprint.

Hotel Vancouver

Hotel Vancouver★

900 W. Georgia St., between Burrard and Hornby Sts. 604-684-3131. www.fairmont.com/hotelvancouver.

A city icon, the "Hotel Van" is one of the continent-wide chain of massive, château-style hotels built by Canadian railroad companies in the late 19C and early 20C. Its **copper roof** and gabled tower are often photographed to symbolize Vancouver.
Built by the **Canadian National Railway** and opened in 1939, the hotel was later taken over by Canadian Pacific; it's now operated by the Fairmont chain, which invested millions of dollars in renovations in the 1990s. Special attention was devoted to the brushed-metal and glass Art Moderne touches in the lobby, which is worth a visit just to experience the atmosphere in one of the world's landmark hotels *(see Hotels)*.

Law Courts and Robson Square★

800 Robson St., between Hornby and Howe Sts.

The Babylonian-style hanging gardens, suspended pools and waterfall freshets of this seven-storey complex make it hard to grasp the fact that it is indeed a single building. And despite its aesthetic appeal, serious business does take place inside this structure housing the provincial law courts ("law courts" is a term for **courthouse**).
Designed by Arthur Erickson, the facility you see here today was not the one originally intended for this site. A massive 55-storey tower was planned in the early 1970s, but never realized. The hundreds of workers, visitors and residents you'll see enjoying the Law Courts' **outside spaces** on a sunny day can attest to the wisdom of that decision.
There's also an **ice rink** for winter skating, and small garden patches at various levels with something in bloom virtually year-round.

LANDMARKS

Sun Tower

100 W. Pender St.

Newspaper publisher Louis Taylor aimed for extravagance with this towering edifice. At 17 storeys, it was tallest in the British Empire for a brief two years, from 1912 to 1914; the copper dome is an example of Beaux Arts design. And the nine half-clad buxom maidens (caryatids) that adorn the top storeys, where gargoyles are usually found, were meant to prick modest Edwardian sensibilities. They did.

Marine Building★

355 Burrard St. at Hastings.

Money was no object for the builders of this elaborate structure, who intended it to be one of the snazziest buildings in North America. Sightseers who still gawk at it agree they succeeded: the terra-cotta frieze over the entrance, the phantasmagoric "Mayan" tilework in the lobby, the massive, figured-brass elevator doors—all are palatial in colour and form and sing of a bygone day when style was as important as function (or budget).

When it opened in 1930, the 21-storey building was the tallest in the British Commonwealth; today it's overshadowed by modern office towers, but none can match its flair. Exterior ornamentation illustrates Vancouver's maritime history, with clipper ships and marine creatures such as sea horses crowding the **entranceway frieze**. The blue, green and maroon tile and brass **lobby** is a fanciful representation of the inside of a Mexican temple. It could be said that the whole thing was a fanciful business enterprise—the structure was finished at $2.3 million, almost 100 percent over budget. Its builders quickly went broke, and the Marine Building was sold to the Guinness family for $900,000 in 1933. A mosaic in the lobby floor depicts the Zodiac—you might say the building was born under a bad sign—in the midst of the Great Depression. Today it's a historic jewel.

Orpheum Theatre★

884 Granville St.
See Performing Arts.

Former Eaton Building

701 Granville St. at Robson St.
604-685-7112.

This massive 1970s building is monumental in several ways. Its bulbous, light-shaded tubular shape has earned it a nickname drawn from classic literature: the "Great White Whale." It was the downtown **Eaton store** until that longtime Canadian chain went bankrupt in 1999. Sears took it over, and reconfigured the Eaton retail persona, which quickly flopped. Sears is moving out, and **Pacific Centre** plans to redevelop the space *(see Pacific Centre p50)*. An industrious Irishman, one **Timothy Eaton**, immigrated to Canada when he was 22 years old. In 1869 he opened his first department store, locating it in Toronto and offering a new incentive to customers—the **money-back guarantee**. Before long, he established a second store

Vancouver as Stand-in

With a constant stream of film and TV productions in the Vancouver area, many city landmarks have served as sets for films—often standing in for other structures of various sorts. The **Vancouver Art Gallery**, for instance, was used as the courtroom for the key scenes in *The Accused*, in which Jodie Foster won her first Academy Award. **Gastown** was transformed into Helena, Montana, for *Legends of the Fall*, with Brad Pitt and Anthony Hopkins. The **Hotel Vancouver**'s green copper roofs became European in the film *Russian Roulette*. And, of course, a West End apartment house was Agent Sculley's Washington, DC, home during the eight-year run of the popular TV show *The X-Files*. The Vancouver area landscape also serves to represent locales around the world when Hollywood comes calling. Most famously, the deep woods around **Hope**, at the east end of the Lower Mainland, were the setting for *First Blood*, the kick-off film in the Rambo series that helped make Sylvester Stallone an international star.

in Toronto as well as a mail-order business, and the chain spread from there. The holiday season brought wonderful **mechanized displays** in Eaton department store windows. In 1905, Eaton's introduced its Santa Claus Parade, which became the largest parade in North America by the 1950s, televised to a world audience of some 30 million viewers.

Holy Rosary Cathedral

646 Richards St. at Dunsmuir St. 604-682-6774. Open Mon–Sat 6am–6pm, Sun 7:30am–9pm.

Once the tallest fir on the early Vancouver skyline occupied this spot. Now a 66m/217ft **steeple** holds its place, and the 15 large **stained-glass windows** dapple light inside much as old-growth woods do. One of the windows *(to the left of the altar)* was actually made in Paris in 1896, before the church was built.
The Gothic Revival-style building was finished in 1900, and declared a cathedral 16 years later. Pope

John-Paul II sang Mass here in 1984; a contrast is presented by the small army of street people who spread their sleeping bags beneath the open atrium on the cathedral's south side.

Sinclair Centre

757 W. Hastings St., at Granville St. www.sinclaircentre.com.

Four historic buildings were melded into a modern shopping complex in this exemplary adaptation. The old Post Office

The Pendulum

HSBC Building, Georgia and Hornby Sts. www.885west georgia.com. Shades of Edgar Allen Poe. One of the best-known pieces of public art in Vancouver, this 15m/50ft-long brushed-steel sculpture swings above the three-storey atrium lobby of the building's namesake bank. Vancouver artist Alan Storey created the piece in 1985.

LANDMARKS

(1910), Customs Warehouse, Federal Building and Winch Building—all imposing Edwardian stone structures—have been joined by an interior **atrium-courtyard** that houses shops and cafes. Among the 20 retail stores is the classy, upscale fashion boutique **Leone**.

Pacific Centre

700 W. Georgia St., at Granville St.
www.pacificcentre.ca.

Two blocks south, Pacific Centre is the modern version of the Sinclair Centre. It is an entirely underground **shopping mall** with 100 shops that stretches three city blocks north and south between Granville and Howe streets. Theoretically, guests at the Four Seasons Hotel need never go outside to shop. The mall's anchor store is **Holt Renfrew**, an upscale apparel chain *(604-681-3121; www.holtrenfrew.com)*, and a huge food court supplies nourishment to hungry shoppers. Pacific Centre is in the process of redeveloping the adjacent former Eaton Building *(Granville St. at Robson St.)* into a mixed-use complex that will include office space and a new three-level **Nordstrum's** department store.

Olympic Cauldron

1055 Canada Place, Vancouver waterfront, next to the Convention Centre.

This spectacular 10-metre-high **Olympic torch** was lit by Canadian hockey legend, Wayne Gretzky, at the opening ceremony of the 2010 Winter Olympics; it stands as a monument to the Games, and a point of artistic fascination on the waterfront. Situated in Jack Poole Plaza, the space and Cauldron are dedicated to Jack Poole, chairman of the board for the Vancouver Olympic Committee. Sadly, Poole died in 2009 and never witnessed the fruits of his efforts.

Olympic Village Seawall

False Creek, Creekside Park.

Built to aid pedestrian movement during the 2010 "Sea to Sky" Winter Games in 2010, the seawall could just as appropriately have been called the "sea walk." Linking neighbourhoods from Granville Island to the Yaletown seawall connection, the 3.84km (2.38mi) path is a scenic paradise for cyclists, joggers and walkers, passing by Science World British Columbia, the Olympic athlete residences (now condominiums), and along False Creek.

LANDMARK BRIDGES

Burrard Street Bridge

Burrard St., crossing False Creek.

This five-lane 1932 Art Deco-style span over **False Creek** comprises an arched gateway to downtown Vancouver. The decorative frieze on the stucco arch reads "By Land and Sea We Prosper."
Stroll across the bridge at sunset to enjoy the expansive **views** of the western horizon and sundown light on the glass towers along False Creek. Residents and knowledgeable visitors use the bridge, and the south end of Burrard Street, as a shortcut to the airport and the highway to Seattle,

Aerial view of Lions Gate Bridge and Stanley Park

©Robert Simon/iStockphoto.com

bypassing the retail congestion of South Granville Street.

Lions Gate Bridge

North end of Stanley Park Causeway, linking Vancouver to the North Shore, crossing the Burrard Inlet.

It's hard to believe, today, that this soaring structure was built with private funds. The **Guinness family** used proceeds from their brewing enterprises to provide access to North Shore property developments, opening the bridge in 1938.

The BC government bought it for $6 million in 1963, and at the end of the 20C, the span's increasing inability to handle all the traffic spurred numerous proposals to replace or expand it—ranging from adding another deck to building a tunnel beneath the entire downtown Vancouver peninsula. In the end, superficial improvements were made, and all other plans abandoned.

Today traffic crosses on three reversible lanes. The suspension bridge's main span stretches 472m/1,440ft, and the deck sits 61m/180ft above the water. It's also called the **First Narrows** bridge, after the passage it crosses. In 2005, the Government of Canada declared the Lions Gate Bridge a National Historic Site.

Second Narrows Bridge

On Hwy. 1, across Burrard Inlet at the second narrows.

This six-lane lift bridge (the highway is balanced out over the water, rather than suspended from cables) was built in 1960. It spans some 323m/1,060ft. During construction a part of the north arm span collapsed, killing 18 workers; in 1994 the bridge was renamed the **Ironworkers Memorial Bridge**.

Its original name (still in common use) refers to the fact that it crosses the second neck in Burrard Inlet; the Lions Gate Bridge spans the first. The 1925 dedicated railway lift bridge runs parallel to it.

Capilano Suspension Bridge

See Nearby Vancouver.

51

MUSEUMS

The unique history and culture of Pacific Canada are what distinguish Vancouver's best museums—Native totems and crafts, seafaring history, singular artworks that depicts the stunning BC landscape. The number of noteworthy museums in Vancouver may be modest, but you'll find collections here that you won't find anywhere else on earth.

UBC MUSEUM OF ANTHROPOLOGY★★★

6393 N.W. Marine Dr., on the University of British Columbia campus. 604-822-5087. www.moa.ubc.ca. Open mid-May–early Oct daily 10am–5pm (Tue until 9pm). Rest of the year Tue–Sun 10am–5pm (Tue until 9pm). Closed Dec 24 & 25. $17; Tue eve $9.

Known the world over for its vast collection of aboriginal works—and the sensational building that houses them—the Museum of Anthropology (MOA) is one of North America's most important cultural institutions. It's also a great place to spend an afternoon looking at wonderful things. Designed by renowned Canadian architect Arthur Erickson, the cast-concrete building rests atop a bluff overlooking the Strait of Georgia. From the outside, its huge concrete frame mimics a First Nations longhouse. As you descend a ramp into the main gallery, the roof rises, providing ever-taller halls for the totems that form the centrepiece of the museum's 38,000-item collection.

Great Hall

The museum's main gallery boasts ground-to-ceiling curtain-glass walls that let in every bit of available daylight. Massive **totems** draw your attention first—almost all the Northwest Coast First Nations are represented, but the most prominent are the Haida, Kwakwaka'wakw, Nisga'a and Coast Salish, in whose hands the art of carving totems reached its peak in the late 19C. Ravens,

UBC Museum of Anthropology

©Leslie Forsberg/Michelin

Raven and the First Men (1980) by Bill Reid
©Leslie Forsberg/Michelin

whales, eagles, salmon, bears, wolves and countless other creatures carved into the cedar logs demonstrate the Native peoples' affinity for the natural world that sustained them. **Smaller pieces**—bentwood cedar boxes, plaited-reed baskets, ceremonial masks—show the skill of figured designs that make Northwest Coast art distinctive.

Visible Storage Galleries

You'll find one of the world's most important collections of aboriginal artifacts here. Almost 14,000 objects are displayed in cases for visitors to see, in what the museum calls "visible storage."

Koerner Ceramics

This glistening 600-plus piece collection of European ceramics poses an intriguing contrast to the massive—both are beautiful and skillfully made, but utterly different in style.

Bill Reid Rotunda

The museum is also the most important repository for the work of famed **Haida artist** Bill Reid *(see sidebar, below)*. Reid helped create some of the poles and longhouses outside the museum in its representation of a traditional **coast village**. Stroll these paths, past alder groves, with totems peering down, and sense the silent spirits that inhabit BC's coast. Inside, small and large pieces include a fine selection of Reid's **jewellery,** and a **canoe** carved in the traditional fashion, with placards showing how it was done. Lustrous and haunting, **Raven and the First Men** is the work universally considered Reid's masterpiece. A depiction of the Haida creation myth, this sculpture has its own separate gallery at the museum. Reid carved it from a four-ton cedar block, and it was dedicated by Prince Charles in 1980. The work rests in a bed of sand brought by the Haida people from the beach in the Haida Gwaii

Bill Reid

A Canadian national treasure, Bill Reid (1920–1998) is one of those artists whose work is firmly rooted in his cultural heritage, but transcends it completely. The Haida are the ancestral people of Haida Gwaii (formerly the Queen Charlotte Islands), whose mist-clad, high-timbered shores evoke both the forces of nature and the spirits of vanished lifestyles. Reid was born in Victoria (his mother was Haida) and paid little attention to his heritage until he visited his grandfather in the islands in 1943. That visit fired his interest in traditional Haida carving, and he abandoned a career in radio. Reid's 40-year life as an artist encompassed works both big—totems and canoes—and small, such as finely-wrought gold and silver jewellery. His pieces reside in collections around the world, but his fame rests on the large works he did on commission late in life. A massive sculpture of a canoe bearing the earth's creatures decorates the International Terminal at Vancouver International Airport; a breaching killer whale greets visitors to Vancouver Aquarium; and a huge wooden bear sits in the Museum of Anthropology's Great Hall.

Islands, where, according to Haida legend, on this very sand the Raven opened the clamshell in which humanity huddled, freeing the first men to discover the world. A recent addition (2012) to the Bill Reid Rotunda is a donation of 11 intricate pieces of **gold and silver jewellery** that the artist crafted from 1954 to 1974; they exemplify his experimentation with European goldsmithing techniques.

🏛 MUSEUM OF VANCOUVER★★

1100 Chestnut St., in Vanier Park. 604-736-4431. www.museumof vancouver.ca. Open Jul–Aug daily 10am–5pm (Thu until 8pm). Rest of the year Tue–Sun 10am–5pm. Closed Dec 25. $12.

A huge **stainless-steel crab** stands at the entrance to the city's oldest museum. Sculptor George

Museum of Vancouver

MUST SEE

Family Fun at the Museum of Vancouver

The Museum of Vancouver offers **special programs** for family enjoyment. Here are suggested activities for some of the permanent exhibits that make for a fun day for families at the museum:

1930s-1940s: Kids and their parents can be children all over again as they play with toys from yesteryear, comparing toys of that era to modern ones, and even having a go at making olden-day toys.

1950s - The 50s Gallery: Like the rest of the post-war world, Vancouver had toned down certain expectations and adjusted its goals to the sensibility of the "new frontier" and a return to core values. Find out how Vancouver's avenues, formerly dominated by street cars, were remade to accommodate the new propensity toward personal vehicles, and watch those controversial neon lights take over the town. Learn how up-and-coming neighbourhoods were established, and what went on at night in Gastown.

1960s-1970s You Say You Want a Revolution: Try on a few psychedelic hippie costumes. Parents can explain to their kids why they (or their parents) engaged in local and large-scale rebellion. Largely thanks to its moderate climate, Vancouver drew hippies from across Canada—and the world—as their gathering place; they left an indelible mark that exists today. You'll be surprised to learn that upscale Kitsilano was once a hippie haven with a peace symbol on every door. Check out the history of enviro-friendly groups like Greenpeace and how they got their start here back in the groovy days.

Norris fashioned it to symbolize the creature that guards the harbour in First Nations lore. Inside, the city's Native traditions and modern history come to life through a collection of some 70,000 items, ranging from First Nations ceremonial masks and 5,500 toy soldiers to neon signs from Vancouver's heyday as a capital of this commercial art. Founded in 1894, the Museum of Vancouver now shares a complex with the **H.R. MacMillan Space Centre★** (see For Kids); the building's cone-shaped roof mimics a Salish cedar rain-hat. Permanent collections are displayed in decades, making it easy to explore the last century of Vancouver life.

Neon Vancouver/ Ugly Vancouver

The neon sign collection is a campy, almost creepy throwback to the days of Vancouver's flashy big-city lights of the 1950s, 60s and 70s. The diverse assemblage evokes the former controversy over Vancouver's self-image. During the three decades in question, Vancouver hosted as many as 19,000 neon signs, a truly blinding array. Supporters of the glitz believed the signs embodied **big-city glamour**; detractors said they cheapened Vancouver and eclipsed its natural beauty. Witness for yourself Vancouver's public persona as portrayed in neon **retail signs** like Chez Paris, the Drake Hotel and Owl Drugstore, in every color, size and typeface.

1900s-1920s: The Gateway to the Pacific

Like today, Vancouver of the early 20C saw lifestyle hype, inflated real estate and vast cultural diversity. During this three-decade window, Vancouver evolved from its modest roots to **big-city status**. The street-car network was expanding, allowing new residential enclaves access to the city's core. Despite the prejudices that typified the era, the world, especially Asians, came to Vancouver's doorstep, seeking new beginnings. Period costumes, documents, photographs, models and artifacts make concrete the city's "golden years" as well as its **economic challenges** and the coming of World War I in 1914.

1930s-1940s: Boom, Bust, and War

Black and white photographs, artifacts, documents and re-created settings enliven topics such as the **city's origin** and the financial **crash of 1929**. In that same year, Vancouver merged with the neighbouring towns of South Vancouver and Point Grey to create Canada's third-largest city.

Discover a Vancouver in the throes of economic depression. Saved by Canada's involvement in World War II in 1939, and the resulting economic upswing, the country found its factories and shipyards productive again. But the war threatened Japanese residents of Canada with internment camps.

1950s: The 50s Gallery

Exhibits reflect the breezy lifestyle of Vancouverites in the post-war era. Check out the re-created **living room** setting complete with a TV and other "modern" amenities. Displays of **period clothing** call to mind Betty Crocker attired in apron, skirt and high heels. Play tunes on the large **jukebox** and 45RPM vinyl records. Recall the days of soda fountains and Chubby Checker when you visit this space.

1960s-1970s: You Say You Want a Revolution

Tie-dyed clothing, fringed and beaded, brings visitors back to the two decades of the **love, peace and freedom movement**. T-shirts, posters, banners and buttons capture the essence of the protest

Neon Vancouver, Museum of Vancouver

©Museum of Vancouver

Vancouver Art Gallery

era. Hear rock songs and see films about rock bands of the time.

VANCOUVER ART GALLERY★★

750 Hornby St., at Robson St. 604-662-4719. www.vanartgallery. bc.ca. Open daily 10am–5pm (Tue until 9pm and late May–Sept Sun until 9pm). Closed Jan 1 & Dec 25. $20; Tue eve by donation.

This stately building is Pacific Canada's leading art institution: it represents the work of BC's two best-known architects, and it has the largest collection of the province's most famous artist—**Emily Carr** *(see sidebar)*. Designed by **Francis Rattenbury**, designer of Victoria's Parliament Buildings in *(see Excursions)*, the structure served as the Vancouver Courthouse from 1911 to 1974. It was recast in 1983 as an art museum by **Arthur Erickson**, who transformed the **rotunda** into a core of light along the centre of the building. Hung here are works by modern BC artists such as Stan

Emily Carr

Born in Victoria, Emily Carr (1871–1945) found her greatest success in the more cosmopolitan Vancouver, where she lived for a while as a young woman, and formed her lifelong disdain for artistic and social convention. The city's art museum was one of the few institutions to show her work during her lifetime, so when Carr died she willed almost all her works to the Art Gallery, which hangs a rotating selection of about two dozen canvases. Carr's brooding, dark-hued portraits of her homeland's rain forests, and the vanishing aboriginal life within them, are so distinctive that her paintings are instantly recognizable. Much of her work depicts First Nations life and draws its style from that motif—*Big Raven*, for instance, resembles the raven's representations on totem poles. Carr is often classed with Frida Kahlo and Georgia O'Keeffe, artists with whom she shared personal and cultural perspectives.

MUSEUMS

Douglas, Rodney Graham and Jeff Wall, as well as works by Carr and Group of Seven artists.

Grounds for Dissension

The museum **grounds** are as dynamic as the art inside. Various parts of the building and its plaza and fountains outside have served as the settings for innumerable films. The steps on the southwest corner, facing Robson, are ground zero for protests in Western Canada—virtually no topic is too trifling for someone to set up a soapbox here; major controversies draw hundreds of demonstrators.

VANCOUVER MARITIME MUSEUM★★

1905 Ogden Ave., in Vanier Park. 604-257-8300. www.vancouver maritimemuseum.com. Open Victoria Day–Labour Day daily 10am–5pm. Rest of the year Tue– Sun 10am–5pm. $11.

Vancouver's museum devoted to its maritime history sits,

appropriately, on the shoreline at the entrance to False Creek. It offers an intriguing survey of the boats that plied the Northwest Coast, the people who sailed them and the reasons they did so. The museum was built as a BC centennial project in 1958.

St. Roch

The tent-like roof of the building shields the mast of a Royal Canadian Mounted Police patrol ship that was first to traverse the **Northwest Passage** through Canada's Arctic in both directions. Amazingly enough, despite its career bashing through icy waters, the St. Roch is a **wood-hulled boat**—and a small one, at just 32m/104ft, built in a Vancouver shipyard in 1928. The schooner is permanently dry-docked inside the museum. You can clamber into and through the ship, marveling at the incredibly tight quarters its 10-man crew occupied while battling the Arctic during the ship's unprecedented World War

St. Roch, Vancouver Maritime Museum

©Leslie Forsberg/Michelin

Vancouver Maritime Museum

©Leslie Forsberg/Michelin

Shipping Today

A tugboat **pilothouse** represents present-day seafaring; the tug's wheel sits ready for children to turn. Exhibits explain the modern operations of Canada's busiest port.

H.R. MACMILLAN SPACE CENTRE★

See For Kids.

LANGLEY CENTENNIAL MUSEUM

9135 King St., in Fort Langley, just southwest of Fort Langley National Historic Site. 604-532-3536. www.langleymuseum.org. Open Mon–Sat 10am–4:45pm, Sun 1pm–4:45pm. Entry by donation.

Opened in 1958, the museum is a repository of artifacts that document the cultural heritage of the town and its people. Be sure to see the re-created **general store** and the excellent collection of **First Nations arts** and artifacts.

ROEDDE HOUSE MUSEUM

See Historic Sites.

ll voyages. The first of these trips, from Vancouver to Halifax, took two years (1940–1942), during which the ship was twice trapped in sea ice.

Exploration History

In the rest of the museum, you'll discover Vancouver's lifelong ties to maritime affairs, from the canoes carved out of cedar by Native peoples to the late-18C Northwest voyages of European explorers. **Ship models** and descriptive exhibits and installations (the forecastle of a sailing ship, Captain George Vancouver's *Discovery*) illustrate often-rugged life at sea.

 Centennial Pole

In a small plaza south of the Maritime Museum, Vanier Park.
Not only is this majestic totem one of the finest works of famed carver Chief **Mungo Martin** (1879–1962), it was once the world's tallest. Martin carved it for the BC centennial in 1958, at which time the 30.5m/100ft pole reigned supreme. It was later superseded by a pole in Victoria, which was in turn surpassed by a pole erected in 2002 in Alert Bay on Vancouver Island. The 10 clan symbols on the Centennial Pole depict the 10 bands of Martin's Kwakwaka'wakw people.

HISTORIC SITES

Historic site or venerable landmark? Considering Vancouver's colourful history, it's sometimes hard to categorize. We've included a few historic must-sees here, but check out Chinatown as well as the Landmarks chapter for more great places with a past.

GASTOWN★

Water St., between Carrall and Richards Sts.

Vancouver's original site is now a **historic district** with a split personality: housed in a fine collection of 19C buildings is a hodge-podge of 20C curio shops, art galleries, restaurants and stores. The city's first **timber mills** began cutting wood here from nearby forests in 1862; many of the brick and stone buildings in Gastown incorporate superstructures of old-growth Douglas fir timbers. Rundown and slated for "urban renewal" by the 1950s, the area was revived and renovated thanks to citizen activism in the early 1970s. The provincial government designated Gastown a historic district in 1971. Gastown was designated a Canadian National Historic Site in 2009.

"Gassy" Jack

Pioneer life stories (or legends) have a tendency to be colourful, and Gassy Jack's is no exception. Born in 1830 in England, **Jack Deighton** went to sea at 14. He eventually wound up in the new colony of British Columbia, where he opened a saloon in New Westminster, up the Fraser River from present-day Vancouver. When that failed, he loaded a canoe with a bottle of whisky, a few sticks of furniture and a yellow dog and paddled to Burrard Inlet, where he began selling whisky to loggers at the new mill. In 1867 thirsty loggers helped him build the Globe Saloon—in 24 hours as legend has it—and Deighton's bar thrived. His nickname? Supposedly it refers to his never-failing willingness to tell a tale. A **statue** of Deighton stands in Maple Tree Square at Carrall and Water Streets.

Hotel Europe, Gastown

©Atlantide SNC/age fotostock

Interior, Waterfront Station

©SuperStock/age fotostock

Notable Buildings in Gastown

Byrnes Block
Water St., between Carrall and Abbott Sts.
An 1886 brick edifice decked out with pediments and pilasters, this block-long structure has several distinctions—it was one of the city's first brick buildings, and it occupies the site on which "Gassy" Jack Deighton built his second saloon.

Steam Clock

One of the most-photographed icons in Vancouver, this clock may look historic—indeed its mechanism harks back to the early Victorian era when steam powered all machinery—yet the Gastown clock is a modern artifact. It was built in 1977, representing a capstone to the district's restoration. The **whistle**, which sounds every quarter-hour, is steam-driven, but the clock is electric.

Gaoler's Mews
Water and Carrall Sts., across Water St.
The 19C customs house and jail now houses several First Nations art galleries.

Hotel Europe
Carrall and Water Sts., east of Maple Tree Square.
This 1908 poured-concrete structure no longer operates as a hotel, but it is one of the first of its kind in North America. All modern construction is required to blend with the district's heritage buildings.

WATERFRONT STATION

601 W. Cordova St., 604-953-3333. www.translink.ca.

Completed in 1914 this handsome, red-brick building overlooking Burrard Inlet, near Gastown, was once the passenger terminal for **Canadian Pacific Railway**. Its facade is distinguished by a colonade and entryway of columns with Ionic capitals. The expansive flat roof is ringed by a balustrade. After extensive renovation beginning in 1977, the station was transformed into a modern intermodal transportation facility. Today it serves as a departure point for SeaBus, SkyTrain and other Translink modes of transportation. Be sure to step inside the main concourse to view the **panels** painted with historic scenes of rail travel through Canada long ago. From here, a popular destination, Lonsdale Quay's **public market**, can be reached by a SeaBus ride across the harbor.

ROEDDE HOUSE MUSEUM

Barclay and Broughton Sts., West End. 604-684-7040. www.roeddehouse.org. Open for tours year-round; call for longer hours and special occasions in summer. Open May–Aug daily 10am–4pm. Rest of the year daily 1pm–4pm. $5; $8 for Sun afternoon tea and tour.

Quiet **Barclay Heritage Square**— just one-block in size—and the neighbourhood surrounding it hint at the genteel quality of life that existed in Vancouver's **West End** a century ago.

The highlight of this area is the opulent, fully restored 1893 Queen Anne Revival-style mansion, Roedde House. Built for Vancouver bookbinder Gustav Roedde and his family, the house is thought to have been designed by Francis Rattenbury, the architect responsible for the Parliament Buildings and the Empress Hotel in Victoria (*see Excursions*). The home's most distinctive feature is its rooftop **cupola**. It was from here, at the end of the 19C, that residents could watch the sea lanes for incoming vessels. Now, alas, West End development has blocked the view.

The 11 rooms in the **interior** of the house are furnished to depict the middle-class lifestyle of an immigrant family in the late 19C. In the adjacent park you'll find a **Victorian garden**; visit in spring (*Mar–Jun*) to see the blooms of dozens of mature rhododendrons cascade down the huge bushes like coloured waterfalls.

Parlour, Roedde House Museum

©Jessica Gryp/Roedde House Museum

MUST SEE

Forbidden Vancouver walking tour

City Walking Tours

One of the most popular tours for visitors to Vancouver and local history buffs is **Forbidden Vancouver**, a stroll through memory lane to spots like Gastown and Chinatown of the early 20th century. Walkers follow "undercover newspaper reporter" Will Woods as he literally takes them through the **back alleys** of the city, and reveals its seedy side from long ago. Using wit and his penchant for history, England-born Woods, dressed in period costume as a journalist, informs and inspires by engaging walkers in the sordid stories that got him banned as a journalist way back when. Get there early; tours are limited to about 20 people.

Two-hour tours depart from Cathedral Square at Dunsmuir and Richards Sts. Tue–Sat at 6:30pm. $21.50; not recommended for children. www.forbiddenvancouver.ca.

A stop on AIBC tour

Wondering where the waterfront used to be in Yaletown, or why Francis Rattenbury had to hastily leave BC for England despite his fame as an architect? To learn the answer to these and other mysteries of history, take one of the guided walking tours Jul–early Sept *(10am and 1pm; about 2hrs; $10)* of Vancouver's (and Victoria's) neighbourhoods offered by the **Architectural Institute of British Columbia** *(604-683-8588; www.aibc.ca/pub_resources/aibc_outreach/architectural_walking_tour.html)*. Check the website for a schedule of departing times and locations.

HISTORIC SITES

PARKS AND GARDENS

Green space is everywhere in Vancouver and its surrounding suburbs—little half-block play areas, undeveloped outlying parcels of wetland or woods. It's the big city parks that get the most attention, though. Recreational areas like Stanley Park and the provincial parks on the North Shore offer gardens and places to play galore, along with a vast array of attractions ranging from gourmet restaurants to beaches.

STANLEY PARK★★★

At the northwest end of downtown, access via Georgia and Davie Sts. 604-257-8400. www.city.vancouver. bc.ca/parks. Open 24hrs daily.

Stanley Park is the unquestioned highlight of Vancouver, one of North America's best city parks. Urban residents are not only justifiably proud of their famous park, they use it avidly—and visitors are just as fond of the park's attractions. It's big (405ha/1,000 acres), beautiful, accessible and uncrowded. A visit to Stanley Park can be as simple as a 20minute stroll along the **seawall** path. Or it can be as elaborate as an interactive sea-mammal experience at the **Vancouver Aquarium★★★** (*see For Kids*), followed by a walk

through **deep forests** to an elegant dinner at a restaurant overlooking the Strait of Georgia. Stanley Park has wildlife, woods, sandy beaches, children's play areas, statues and **totems**, gardens and pools. Film crews use the park as a stand-in for woods worldwide.

You can accomplish a quick **driving tour** (*see Scenic Drive*) of the park in a morning, following the counterclockwise drive that skirts its perimeter and touches on most of the high points. However, it's best to set off **on foot**, since much of the park's finest territory lies beyond the roadway.

It's commonly assumed that Stanley Park's acres of Western red cedar, Douglas fir and western hemlock are old-growth forest. They're not; most of the park

Stanley Park

©City of Vancouver

A Park for the People?

In the late 19C Vancouver's first city council asked the federal government to preserve the land for Stanley Park and deed it to the city; it had been a military reserve, but it was not untouched forest. The transfer took place in 1888, and the park was dedicated the following year by its namesake, **Lord Peter Stanley**, Canada's governor-general. Though the city's founders showed amazing foresight to preserve such a magnificent piece of land, their motives were not wholly altruistic: the park was meant to boost the viability of housing developments in the West End.

was logged before 1870 ("high-graded"—only the biggest and best timber was removed). The nearest true old-growth forest is across Burrard Inlet at **Lighthouse Park★★**. However, logging ceased so long ago in Stanley Park that much of its forest is now approaching maturity. As you hike and bike along some of the interior trails, you'll see some impressively large trees—despite the loss of thousands of trees in a violent wind storm in December 2006.

Visiting Stanley Park

It's best to arrive by bus or on foot, as **parking** poses a problem; even if you can find a space, it costs up to $3 per hour (the pay meters must be fed; parking police are vigilant). Popular Vancouver Aquarium, Totem Park, Prospect Point, Third Beach and Second Beach are the most crowded. If you can, arrive early, find parking along Stanley Park Drive, the circumferential road, and walk to the sights. A stroll from Third Beach to the Aquarium, for example, takes just 15 to 20 minutes.

Other Tips

◆ Stop first at the **visitor centre,** which is located about .8km/.5mi in on Stanley Park Drive near the aquarium entrance, and grab a map.

◆ Do not feed the cute squirrels, raccoons and other critters—they are wild and they do bite.

◆ If you want to swim, **Second Beach★** is best in the morning; Third Beach is best in the afternoon.

◆ Use the free **park shuttle bus**: its makes 15 stops at popular destinations (*10am–6:30pm*).

Nature House

South side of Lost Lagoon, at northwest end of Robson St. 604-257-8544. www.stanleyparkecology.ca. Open Jul–Aug Tue–Sun 10am–5pm. Sept–Jun weekends 10am–4pm.

This compact facility is an interpretive centre for Stanley Park, operated by a local ecology organization. Periodic programs cover everything from the creatures that live in the lagoon to the life cycle of the old-growth forest that Stanley Park is becoming again. Volunteers are on-site to answer questions about the park and distribute information.

Scenic Drive★

The 10km/6mi drive that circles the park perimeter will take you past all of its significant sights. Traffic moves **counterclockwise**, starting at the park entrance at the end of West Georgia Street. Stanley Park Drive first swings around Coal Harbour, passing the Vancouver Rowing Club and Royal Vancouver Yacht Club. Between the two, to the north, is the entrance to the Vancouver Aquarium, and the main park **information kiosk**. A quarter-mile farther rises the park's famed collection of **totem poles★** (*see sidebar*), occupying a site where a Coast Salish village stood 150 years ago.

Nine O'clock Gun

At **Hallelujah Point**, just past the totems, this gun is fired every evening—since 1894—to mark a historic fishing curfew. **Brockton Point** holds a replica of the prow of the *Empress of Japan*, one of the first clipper ships to call at the port of Vancouver. Just past that, the Girl in a Wet Suit **statue**, placed on a rock in 1984, mimics the legendary mermaid sculpture that graces Copenhagen's harbour.

Prospect Point★

The road climbs to a bluff at Prospect Point, offering wide **views★** of the North Shore with snowcapped mountains behind, and across the Strait of Georgia to Vancouver Island. A half-mile farther on, stop at the **Hollow Tree**, a much-photographed cedar stump, to see how many people you can fit inside.

Third Beach★

This broad expanse of golden sand is perfect for picnicking and admiring the views. **Ferguson Point** offers more views from a bluff; and the Stanley Park Pool at **Second Beach★** is packed with sunbathers on warm days (*see Outdoor Fun*). The road winds by the park's excellent **pitch-and-putt** golf course, bypassing **Lost Lagoon** (a slightly brackish pond) to return to Georgia Street.

Stanley Park Seawall★★

Ready for a walk? This marvelous 9.5km/6mi **bike and pedestrian path** was the lifework of stonemason James Cunningham (1878–1963). A 9.5km/5.9mi barrier of 46kg/101-pound granite blocks built over the course of 46 years to withstand the battering of winter storms, the seawall follows much the same route as the driving tour described here, but affords better views. At Prospect Point, watch for **Siwash Rock★**, a small sea stack that, according to Native legend, represents the

> #### Totem Poles★
>
> Carved from cedar logs, totems are traditional Native monuments that depict the animals and spirits central to the First Nations' pantheistic belief systems. Ravens, bears, salmon, eagles, frogs, whales and wolves are common figures. An **interpretive centre** near the totems explains traditional Native village life, and a shop offers guidebooks and posters. Artists represented include Bill Reid (*see Museums*) and Chief Mungo Martin, two legendary Native carvers.

Big Cedar

In the 1950s the National Geographic Society declared a **Western red cedar** on the park's western slope the world's largest. Found along the uphill path from Third Beach to the Hollow Tree, the cedar does not seem all that remarkable as you approach—until you stand at its base and circle the 3.6m/12ft-diameter trunk. The tree died in the 1990s, possibly as a result of topping that was done years before.

Near the Third Beach concession, a **red alder** with four trunks is reckoned to be the largest alder in Canada; and a **big-leaf maple** in the woods southeast of the Hollow Tree is considered the largest such maple in the country. That's a lot of big-treedom in one small area—but imagine what trees might have been here before the park was logged!

The **Hollow Tree** itself, right along Stanley Park Drive a half-mile south of Prospect Point, was once sufficiently big enough that today its shell-like stump is a popular photo op, with groups of people standing inside. Springboard notches on the side mark the place where sawyers stood in the 1870s to bring down this huge cedar.

---

petrified soul of a virtuous member of the Salish tribe.

Gardens

Flower fans will want to visit the lovely formal **rose gardens** (along Pipeline Rd.), which reach their peak in June, and the **rhododendron gardens** (south of Lost Lagoon), where hundreds of different varieties burst into bloom in May and June.

Trails

A dozen well-maintained trails crisscross the interior of the park, offering hikers and bikers the opportunity to find solitude in the woods. **Lake Trail** and **Tatlow Walk** are two of the best; you can access them from Stanley Park Drive near Second Beach.

Carriage Tours

Horse-drawn trolleys depart Coal Harbour parking lot mid-Mar–Oct. *1hr tour $29.99. 604-681-5115. www.stanleyparktours.com.*

Vancouver Aquarium★★★, Children's Farmyard and Miniature Train

See For Kids.

VANDUSEN BOTANICAL GARDEN★★

5251 Oak St. at 37th Ave. 604-878-9274. www.vandusen.org. Open year-round daily: Nov–Dec and Jan–Feb 10am–4pm, Mar 10am–5pm, Apr 10am–6pm, May–Aug 9am–8pm, Sept 10am–7pm, Oct 10am–5pm, Dec Festival of Lights 4:30pm–9pm. Closed Dec 25. Jan–Mar and Oct–Dec $7.75, Apr–Sept $10.75.

Imagine houses filling this lovely spot, instead of the colourful botanical garden. That's what it came perilously close to. Once the site of a golf club for the nearby Shaughnessy mansion district (*see Neighbourhoods*), the land that now holds VanDusen garden was slated to be turned into a

Winter aconite and crocus, VanDusen Botanical Garden

©Raymond Chan Photomedia/VanDusen Botanical Garden

hollies to bamboos, and magnolias to birches. Numerous **theme gardens** scattered about the site include a Japanese meditation garden, an herb garden, a perennial garden, a maze and a fern dell. Among the highlights are the following:

Winter Garden

This collection of fragrant witch hazels, winter hazels and winter-blooming jasmine, as well as hellebores and other exotic off-season bloomers, is enchanting in January and February, belying winter's gray skies.

residential housing development in the 1970s. **Citizen activism** spurred the city to buy the 55-acre piece of rolling ground, and it has since grown into a horticultural showpiece.

The garden's overall purpose is to demonstrate the horticultural possibilities offered by Vancouver's **mild climate**—a notion illustrated by the healthy copse of palms growing beneath mature Douglas firs and cedars by the entrance. The wide variety (7,500 different plants) ensures that something is in bloom almost year-round. The gift shop and bookstore focus on material promoting horticulture in the Lower Mainland. Inside the garden, plantings range from

Canadian Heritage Garden

Native Canadian plants here focus on those that clothed, housed and fed First Nations people and pioneers, ranging from red cedar to Saskatoon berries. Plants from both east and west, and the prairie in between, are included.

QUEEN ELIZABETH PARK★

33rd Ave. and Cambie St. 604-257-8400. www.city.vancouver.bc.ca/parks. Open 24hrs daily.

Heron Lake, VanDusen Botanical Garden

© Nancy Wong /VanDusen Botanical Garden

The highest point in Vancouver, a 154m/505ft hillock, is the pinnacle of this 52.5ha/130-acre park, which spreads across the largely open hillside. Six million visitors a year make Queen Elizabeth the city's second most popular park. The northwest end of the park is an **arboretum** that holds almost all the trees native to Canada, as well as many specimens from Europe and elsewhere in North America. **Nat Bailey Stadium**, on the park's southern end, is the summer home of the Vancouver Canadians, the city's minor-league baseball team (see Practical Information).

Bloedel Floral Conservatory

At the park's high ground sits Bloedel Conservatory, a geodesic-style greenhouse that houses 500 tropical plants and fish, and 100 free-flying birds. Paths wander amid the gardens and aviaries. A plexiglass dome covers one of the largest domed greenhouses in the world.

Quarry Gardens

Occupying a former stone quarry, this multi-level garden with its colourful annuals and wide sweeping lawns brings to mind Victoria's Butchart Gardens, though it's not quite as formal (see Excursions).

Viewpoint

Climb to the city's highest point (154m/505ft) here for a wonderful **panorama★★** of Vancouver to the north, and the North Shore Mountains beyond—including the twin "Lions" peaks for which Lions Gate is named. To the east, you can see the snowy cone of

Seasons Restaurant

In Queen Elizabeth Park at 33rd Ave. and Cambie St. 604-874-8008. www.sequoiarestaurants. com. Mon–Sat opens at 11:30am; Sunday opens for brunch at 10:30 am.

Seasons boasts **views** almost as broad as those from the park's pinnacle. Bill Clinton and Boris Yeltsin had dinner here during their summit in 1993; today, brunch is the most popular meal, with dishes ranging from carrot and ginger soup to poached black cod.

Mount Baker. To the west, the Georgia Strait and the mountains of Vancouver Island loom in the distance.

DR. SUN YAT-SEN CLASSICAL CHINESE GARDEN★

578 Carrall St., Chinatown. 604-662-3207. www.vancouver chinesegarden.com. Open May–mid-Jun and Sept 10am–6pm; late Jun–Aug 9:30am–7pm; Oct–Apr 10am–4:30pm. Dec 24 and 31 10am–3pm. Closed Mon Nov–Apr, closed Dec 25 and Jan 1. $14.

You're bound to find serenity amid the intricately laid patios, elaborately decorated pavilions and carefully positioned rocks of the Sun Yat-Sen garden. The stucco, tile-roofed walls of the compound shelter one of the finest formal gardens in North America. Indeed, this was the first true Ming Dynasty-style garden built in North America.
In 1886 Chinese artisans crossed the Pacific to help create it,

bringing with them classical stone, tile, brick and timber.

Like all Chinese gardens, this one focuses as much on the man-made framework for growing things, as on the plants themselves. Each plant is chosen for its symbolic meaning, and the garden celebrates all **four seasons** with azaleas and trees such as maples, magnolias and evergreens. **Moon gates** and open portals offer artful views into **courtyards** and meditation nooks. Frequent guided tours *(included in price of admission)* explain the painstaking construction and significance of every element, none random.

UBC BOTANICAL GARDEN★

6804 S.W. Marine Dr., on the University of British Columbia campus. 604-822-9666.

www.botanicalgarden.ubc.ca. Open daily 9:30am–5pm. $8, or UBC Museums and Gardens Pass $33.

The largest **rhododendron** collection in Canada—400 varieties—nestles beneath the native hemlock trees in this 28ha/70-acre garden that melds Northwest species with horticultural plants. Theme gardens are scattered throughout the property. The setting, on a bluff overlooking the Strait of Georgia, adds to the pleasure of a visit. At the gift shop, you can buy seeds from some of the plants in the botanical garden; the shop also has gardening books, tools and accessories.

Alpine Garden

Specimens from mountains around the world—from Borneo to

The Palm Gardens

Vancouver's much-acclaimed "mild" climate is given exquisite testimony in several gardens near **English Bay Beach**, at the intersection of Denman and Davie streets. Here city horticulturists have planted several dozen palm trees and other tropical plants (including hardy bananas) that thrive in the protected, south-facing location. Though frosts do occur in the area, the waters of English Bay moderate the cold, and the West End high rises block the chilliest northerly winds. On a sunny summer day, with palm fronds waving in the breeze, you could almost believe you were in the Caribbean.

The Palm Gardens

©Leslie Forsberg/Michelin

The Tao of Gardening

Japanese and classical Chinese gardens have many elements in common—rocks, ponds, carefully placed plants, man-made artifacts such as bridges, courtyards and shelters. How do you tell the difference between the two? Japanese gardens use **natural features** to create meditative spaces, whereas Chinese gardens use artfully designed **meditative spaces** to represent nature. The Sun Yat-Sen garden was built by Chinese artisans using traditional tools, materials, plants and techniques, blending the four **traditional elements**: rocks, water, plants and buildings. Limestone rocks represent mountains, and the three key plants are bamboo, representing resilience; pines, representing strength; and plums, whose blossoms symbolize rebirth. The Taoist **yin-yang** balance is represented by rocks and buildings (yang, or hard), and water, which is the soft, or yin, element.

Russia—are included in one of the largest alpine collections in North America.

Asian Garden

Magnolias (in fact, one of the largest collections on earth), rhododendrons and azaleas predominate in this sprawling garden in the shade of mature conifers.

Food Garden

Bearing everything from kiwis to kohlrabi, the raised beds and fruit borders of this garden illustrate what can be grown in household gardens.

Native Garden

You'll find hundreds of species native to the province in this plot.

Physic Garden

Both old and new medicinal plants are here, from yarrow and rose hips to periwinkle, source of a modern drug used to treat leukemia.

BC Rain Forest Garden

Filled with displays of locally native plants, this collection represents elements of the coastal rain forests of southwestern British Columbia and the Southern Interior Wet-belt.

Carolinian Forest

This new feature of the UBC Botanical Garden exemplifies Canadian and eastern North American deciduous hardwood forests.

A Rhododendron By Any Other Name

Would you be surprised to know that those rhododendrons growing in your yard are related to blueberries? Well, they are. They're also related to azaleas, heather and mountain laurel—all members of the heath family, *Ericaceae*. More than a thousand species have been identified within the genus Rhododendron. Known for their shiny dark green leaves and large bright pink, purple or white flowers, rhododendrons grow all over the world, from the Arctic to the tropics.

Garry Oak

The Garry Oak Meadow and Woodland Garden is a new feature of the UBC Botanical Garden. It is an ecological, sustainable landscape, intended to thrive with minimal intervention.

UBC Greenheart Canopy Walkway

6804 S.W. Marine Dr., on the University of British Columbia campus, in the UBC Botanical Garden. 604-822-4208. www.bontanicalgarden.ubc.ca/canopy-walkway. Open daily 10am–4pm. $20 includes admission to the UBC Botanical Garden.

Situated in the David C. Lam Asian Garden, the Greenheart Canopy Walkway is a 308m/1,010ft **aerial trail** system, the only one of its kind in Canada, that offers an intimate glimpse of the natural wonder of a typical west coast forest canopy ecosystem. This aerial concept sees guests traverse bridges suspended 50ft high, allowing access to the treetops, where they will delight at a thriving diversity of flora and fauna that coats the lofty environment. This is more than a stroll around the trees; it's an experience in interaction with the forest and its inhabitants. *Hourly tours take about 45 minutes and are limited to 20 people per tour; they may be booked in advance.*

NITOBE MEMORIAL GARDEN

S.W. Marine Dr., on the University of British Columbia campus. Enter at Gate 4. 604-878-9274. www.botanicalgarden.ubc.ca/nitobe. Open Apr–Oct 9:30am–5pm. $6.

Inside the walls of this 1ha/2.5-acre enclave you'll find a carefully constructed Japanese garden that focuses on traditional elements of balance and serenity. Paths wander amid ponds, meditation gardens, azaleas, flowering cherries and irises. In the fall, the **Asian maples** bear brilliant crimson and orange leaves. Bridges, benches and carefully placed stones complete the meditative atmosphere.

The garden honours Dr. **Inazo Nitobe** (1862–1933), a diplomat and longtime BC resident devoted to bridging the gap between Japanese and North American cultures.

With its teahouse, the **Tea Garden** inside Nitobe is considered to be one of the most authentic outside Japan. "I am in Japan," proclaimed that country's current emperor when he toured the garden in the 1990s.

PACIFIC SPIRIT REGIONAL PARK

Between 4th Ave. and Marine Dr. in the Point Grey section of Vancouver, also south to Fraser River. Information centre at 4915 W. 16th Ave. 604-224-5739. www.metrovancouver.org .

This sprawling expanse of woods borders Southwest Marine Drive on its approach to the University of British Columbia campus. Its extensive network of **hiking trails** (20km/33mi) and **biking trails** (14km/23mi) includes many paths that lead downhill to the shore of English Bay, offering seclusion and light-dappled forest. Along the way, Pacific Spirit meets **Jericho Beach Park** (a shoreline greenbelt that offers sandy beaches and picnic areas) and farther west toward UBC, **Wreck Beach**, a legendary expanse of sand where clothing is optional. On the more northerly stretches of bluff-bordered pebble shore, you'll have spectacular **views★★** of the North Shore Mountains. With sections spreading south completely across the Point Grey Peninsula, the entire park at 763ha/1,885acres ranks as the **largest green space** in Vancouver—nearly twice as large as Stanley Park. Almost entirely logged in the 19C, it has since sprung up again into a lush, largely deciduous forest in which a dozen kinds of ferns grow in the filtered light. The southeast end of the park includes **Camosun Bog**, a rare example of a once-common peat marshland. A boardwalk allows you to experience the bog without damaging it.

NORTH SHORE PARKS

Here's a list of must-visit parks in North and West Vancouver. For detailed descriptions of individual sites, *see Nearby Vancouver.*

Lighthouse Park★★

Marine Dr., 8km/5mi northwest of downtown via Lions Gate Bridge;
⊙ *Follow Marine Dr. west to Beacon Lane.*

This 79ha/185-acre park harbours one of the area's last major parcels of untouched **old-growth forest**. Its vantage point on a Howe Sound headland means you'll get stunning **views★★★** of Vancouver across the water.

Cypress Provincial Park★

12km/7mi northwest of downtown via Lions Gate Bridge & Hwy. 1 west to Cypress Mountain Rd.

Ski areas, fir and hemlock forests and breathtaking **views★★★** are highlights of the 3,000ha/7,400-acre recreational area.

Lynn Canyon Park★

17km/10.5mi north of Vancouver via Lions Gate Bridge to Hwy. 1.
⊙ *Take the Lynn Valley Rd. exit, turn right on Lynn Valley Rd. and right on Peters Rd. to the park.*

This North Shore gorge boasts a 33m/109ft-long **suspension bridge★** and a spectacular waterfall.

Ambleside Park

6km/4mi north of Vancouver via Lions Gate Bridge and west on Marine Dr.

Locals favour this strip of green space interspersed with sandy beaches that starts at the Capilano River and hugs the shoreline for several miles west.

Capilano River Regional Park

9km/6mi north of Vancouver via Lions Gate Bridge to Hwy. 1 to Capilano Rd. ⊙ *Take the exit for Grouse Mountain and continue north to the park.*

🥾 **Hiking trails** within this 142ha/350-acre regional park cross the river and climb into deep forest.

NEARBY VANCOUVER

If you can tear yourself away from Vancouver proper, it's worth a sojourn to the Lower Mainland. This area stretches from the Strait of Georgia east to Hope and the Cascade Range, bounded on the south by the US border, and on the north by the southern flanks of the towering Coast Mountains.

Here you'll find everything from small, U-pick berry farms to spectacular canyons cutting through mountains. Home to some two million people, the **Lower Mainland** includes the Fraser River Delta, the lower Fraser Valley, and the foothills of both the Coast and Cascade ranges. Though it makes up just two percent of British Columbia's landmass, this region contains half the population of the entire province. Urban growth is a reality these days, but a lot of this land remains pastoral, relying on good soil and mild weather for its agricultural bounty. Much of Western Canada's fresh produce is grown in the region, including BC's well-known hothouse tomatoes.

Touring Tip

The **Lions Gate Bridge** (see *Landmarks*), which joins North and West Vancouver to Vancouver proper via the Stanley Park Causeway, is just three lanes wide. It backs up considerably during the morning and evening commute. Though visitors are usually travelling the opposite direction, counter-commute traffic has only one lane on the bridge, so the trip may be no faster. Allow an extra 30 minutes if you are crossing during morning or evening rush hour.

NORTH AND WEST VANCOUVER

These two communities were developed as suburbs of Vancouver, but have long since established their own identities, with small city centres, their own parks, schools and governments. Residents are fond of pointing out that in one direction they have quick access to one of the great cosmopolitan cities of North America—and in the other, heading up into the **North Shore Mountains**, they have access to the edge of one of the biggest, wildest and most spectacular wilderness areas on the continent. The modern, cliff-hugging, multimillion-dollar mansions that line the shore westward from West Vancouver's downtown represent, perhaps, the most valuable real estate in Canada.

Lighthouse Park★★

Off Marine Dr., 8km/5mi northwest of downtown via Lions Gate Bridge; follow Marine Dr. west to Beacon Lane. 604-925-7200. www.westvancouver.ca. Open year-round daily dawn–dusk.

This protected enclave on **Point Atkinson** at the westernmost end of West Vancouver has three wonderful facets: the Lower Mainland's largest remaining **old-growth forest**, inviting hiking trails that lead through the woods

MUST SEE

Lighthouse Park

© Lijuan Guo / Dreamstime.com

down to the shore, and memorable **views★★★** of Vancouver from the shoreline's rocky headlands. The park's untouched woods have made it a popular location for film crews, for whom it has stood in for forests around the world. It is the best place in the Vancouver area to see old-growth trees.

Old-Growth Forest
Fortunately, the temperate rain forest that now forms part of the park was not logged during Vancouver's development. Today,

the big trees (some up to 500 years old, with diameters approaching 2m/7ft) anchor a classic old-growth ecosystem. Huckleberries, vine maples, scrub oak and red-barked madronas (called arbutus in Canada) fill open spaces where light filters through the conifer canopy overhead.

Hiking in Lighthouse Park
Walking the park's paths, in the serene, light-dappled forest understory, hints at what the entire Lower Mainland was like before

Tree-mendous
Douglas fir isn't really a fir. Western red cedar isn't a true cedar, either. And western hemlock doesn't have anything to do with what Socrates drank. Misidentification and accidents of history have created great confusion over the names of the most prominent forest trees of the Pacific Coast—but there's no confusion over their size, beauty and ecological significance. Douglas firs are usually the biggest, most massive trees with thick, reddish-brown corrugated bark that withstands fire well. They can grow to 91.5m/300ft in height and 3m/10ft in diameter. Red cedars have fabric-like bark, drooping branches and foliage, sturdy flared bases; they favour wetter locations. Western hemlocks have smoother, thinner bark, and lacier foliage than Douglas firs, but approach similar size and age. A true, mature temperate rain forest, like the one in Lighthouse Park, has a mix of all three types, in various sizes and ages.

Howe Sound

© Nina Ignatova/Dreamstime.com

European settlement. The best path through the forest parallels the road on the west side of the peninsula *(follow signs to the outdoor theatre)*. Once you reach the **Point Atkinson Lighthouse** complex, shoreline trails lead both east and west along the rocky headlands.

SEA TO SKY HIGHWAY★★

Rte. 99 runs 102km/63mi from Horseshoe Bay in West Vancouver north to Whistler. Visitor information: www.britishcolumbia.com.

Sights below are organized from south to north.

Even if you don't want to follow Route 99 all the way to Whistler, be sure to drive along at least a part of this highway for incredible **views★★★** of the blue-green waters of the Howe Sound with mountains all around it. Extending some 48km/30mi into the Coast Mountains, this deep fjord provides some of the province's most dramatic coastal scenery between the picturesque ferry port of **Horseshoe Bay** and the town of **Squamish** to the north.

Xá:ytem Interpretive Centre★

In the early 1990s, stone tools found during work for a subdivision near Mission led to the discovery of the remains of an extensive settlement and spiritual site of the Sto:lo people, who lived along the shores of the Fraser River long before Europeans arrived. Today, in the cedar longhouse of the **Xá:ytem Interpretive Centre** *(35087 Lougheed Hwy., Mission; open year-round 9am–4:30pm; $10.50; 604-820-9725; www. xaytem.ca; 2hr tours at 9:30am and 12:30pm),* you can learn how the Sto:lo people flourished in this area. In the hands-on workshops, you can use traditional methods to create your own cedar basket, mat or drum.

MUST SEE

LILLOOET

SEA TO SKY
HIGHWAY

★★★ WHISTLER ① ②
Blackcomb
Wizard Chair ①
Whistler Village Alta L. ②
Whistler Village
Gondola ③
Brandywine
Falls PP ★ Blackcomb Mtn.
Garibaldi ▲ 2439 (8000)
★ Whistler Mtn.
△ 2182 (7160)
.2315 (7593) Spearhead Range
Cheakamus L.
Cheakamus
△ Black Tusk GARIBALDI
Garibaldi L. PP

TANTALUS
PP Highway
99 Mt. Garibaldi
△ 2678 (8784) McBride Range
▲ Diamond Head
▲ The Gargoyles

Ashlu Cr.
Squamish River Valley
Cheakamus
Clowhom

Alice Lake PP
Brackendale Pitt
Lake Douglas

Squamish Stawamus
Chief Monolith Forest
△ 700 (2296)
Shannon Falls ★

Sechelt
Forest Britannia Beach PINECONE-
★ Britannia Mine BURKE
Museum ★★ PP

GOLDEN
Gambier Indian EARS Mt.
Island Judge
Lions Howay
99 Bay Indian PP Park
Langdale ★ Sea to Sky ★ Arm Pitt Lake
Bowen PP
Island Cypress Mt. Coquitlam Alouette
Horseshoe PP Seymour Lake Lake
Bay PP

Stave
Lake

NANAIMO

Coquitlam
7
★★★ VANCOUVER
99
Strait of Burnaby
Georgia Surrey Langley Fort Langley NHS ★
Richmond Centennial
Museum CHILLIWACK
FRASER 7

0 10 mi
0 20 km

BELLINGHAM

HOTELS	RESTAURANTS
The Fairmont Château Whistler......①	Elements Urban Tapas Lounge.........①
Summit Lodge.....................②	Rim Rock Cafe......................②
Whistler Hostel International........③	

Britannia Mine Museum★★

38km/24mi north of Horseshoe Bay on Rte. 99, in Britannia Beach. 604-896-2233. Open daily 9am–5pm. $21.50. www.britanniamine museum.ca.

This former copper mine, now a National Historic Site, enjoyed its heyday beginning in World War I,
when Britain and her allies relied on its output. By 1929 it was the largest copper mine in the British Empire. Closed in 1974, the mine now welcomes visitors who pile into ore cars for a trip into the 671m/2,200ft **supply shaft**. The eerie eight-level **concentrator building** has often served as a film set. Guided tours *(45min)* are highly recommended.

Get Out on the Rivers

Native people and early settlers relied on rivers to get around, but today most people just cross over them or catch fleeting glimpses from their cars. **Fraser River Safari** *(7057 Mershon St., Mission; 604-826-7361; www.FraserRiverSafari.com; year-round $99)* navigates the busy **Fraser River** in its enclosed jet boat through ever-changing shallow gravel bars to the confluence of the clear waters of the **Harrison River** with the turbulent Fraser.

Shannon Falls★★

45km/28mi north of Horseshoe Bay.

A short hike from the site's parking lot along Route 99 leads to a viewing point at the base of these impressive falls, which cascade 335m/1,100ft over a cliff here.

Whistler★★★

See Excursions.

Capilano Canyon★

From Lions Gate Bridge, take Marine Dr. east to Capilano Rd., Exit 14, in North Vancouver. The suspension bridge entrance is at 3735 Capilano Rd. 604-985-7474. www.capbridge.com. Open May–

Sept daily 8:30am–8pm. Rest of the year daily 9am–dusk. Closed Dec 25. $33.95.

To appreciate this deep canyon, take the narrow pedestrian **Capilano Suspension Bridge** *(see below)* 70m/230ft above the Capilano River. This wire-rope bridge, one of the best-known in North America, sways and bounces to the thrill of visitors as they walk across it. The entrance complex is a hodge-podge of knick-knack shops, cafes and exhibits ranging from cigar-store Indians to a history of logging in the area.

🦕 Capilano Suspension Bridge

Some 800,000 visitors enjoy the gorgeous views from this walking bridge that rises 70m/230ft above the river, tucked close to a low mountainside. Because it is integral to a private facility, there is an admission charge.
Built in 1889 and rebuilt in 1956, the bridge measures 137m/450ft, and sways as visitors walk across it. On the opposite side, **Treetops Adventure★** encompasses seven suspension bridges and **viewing platforms** secured, without nails or bolts, to trunks of Douglas firs; some platforms sit 30m/100ft above ground. The new **Cliffwalk** is a series of cantilevered bridges.

Treetops Adventure, Capilano Canyon
©Eric P. Lucas/Michelin

MUST SEE

The view from Grouse Mountain

©Grouse Mountain

Cypress Provincial Park★

12km/7mi northwest of downtown Vancouver via Lions Gate Bridge and Hwy. 1 to Cypress Mountain Rd. 604-926-5612. www.env.gov.bc.ca/bcparks. Open year-round daily.

Clinging to the heights of the **Coast Range** above West Vancouver, this ski and snow sports area was the site of the snowboard and freestyle events during the 2010 Winter Olympics. In summer, 🥾**hiking trails** lead through the western red-cedar and yellow-cedar forests for which the 3,012-hectare/7,440-acre park is named. The access road leads to

Highview Lookout, which permits a breathtaking **view★★** of the Vancouver area.

Grouse Mountain★★

From Lions Gate Bridge, take Capilano Rd. to 6400 Nancy Greene Way, North Vancouver. 604-90-9311. www.grousemountain.com. Aerial tram open year-round daily 9am–10pm; $39.95.

The steep aerial **tram ride** from the base of this attraction rises 1,100m/3,700ft to a ridgeline recreation complex that offers an unmatched **panorama★★** of the Vancouver area. On clear days, the view embraces Vancouver Island, the Fraser delta and Burrard Inlet.

Indian Arm

For a different type of beach experience, try Indian Arm, the southernmost fjord in North America. This long tongue of saltwater stretches from the east end of Burrard Inlet northward into the heart of the Coast Range. Indian Arm quickly passes from its urban beginnings into wilderness, with snowcapped peaks above, waterfalls rushing over stone faces, and sandy coves where emerald waters are just warm enough for the adventurous to take a dip. Both canoeing and kayaking are possible in this protected inlet; **Deep Cove Canoe & Kayak Centre** (*2156 Banbury Rd., North Vancouver; 604-929-2268; www.deepcovekayak.com*) offers rentals and guided tours.

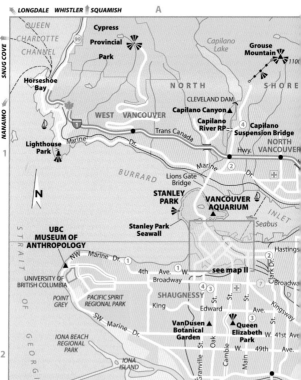

QUEEN
CHARLOTTE
CHANNEL

SNUG COVE

NANAIMO

Cypress
Provincial
Park

Capilano
Lake

Grouse
Mountain

1100

NORTH   SHORE

CLEVELAND DAM

Horseshoe
Bay

Capilano Canyon ▲

Capilano
River RP

WEST   VANCOUVER

Capilano
Suspension Bridge

Trans Canada

NORTH
VANCOUVER

Hwy. (2)

Marine   Dr.

Lighthouse
Park

Marine

Dr.

1

BURRARD

Marine   Dr.

N

Lions Gate
Bridge

STANLEY
PARK

VANCOUVER
AQUARIUM

INLET

Seabus

UBC
MUSEUM OF
ANTHROPOLOGY

Stanley Park
Seawall

Hastings

NW   Marine   Dr. (1)

STRAIT

UNIVERSITY OF
BRITISH COLUMBIA

4th   Ave. (1)
W.
Broadway

see map II

(2)
Clark Dr.

(7)
Broadwa

POINT
GREY

PACIFIC SPIRIT
REGIONAL PARK

SHAUGNESSY

(4)(3)

OF

King

SW   Marine   Dr.

Edward

Kingsway

Ave.

2

GEORGIA

IONA BEACH
REGIONAL
PARK

IONA
ISLAND

VanDusen ▲
Botanical
Garden

Queen
Elizabeth
Park

(3)

W. 41st   Ave.

Granville

Oak

Cambie

Main

W.   49th   Ave.

Knight

Sturgeon
Bank

SEA ISLAND

SEA ISLAND

(99)

LULU

VANCOUVER

map I

Vancouver
International
Airport

Alderbridge
Way

Richmond

0   3 mi
0   5 km

Westminster   Hwy.

RICHMOND

A

Go simply to experience the ride and the view from the top and enjoy a meal on the outdoor patio of the mountaintop **restaurant** (call for reservations), a peerless place to have lunch or dinner on a clear summer day.

Skiing and snow sports are popular in winter, and ▲ **hiking** and ▲ **biking** rule in summer. City

residents flock here in winter to ski. The **Grouse Grind**, an extremely steep climb (3km/2mi) that is one of Vancouver's most popular trails, ascends the mountain.

Lynn Canyon Park★

17km/10.5mi north of Vancouver via Lions Gate Bridge. Take Hwy. 1

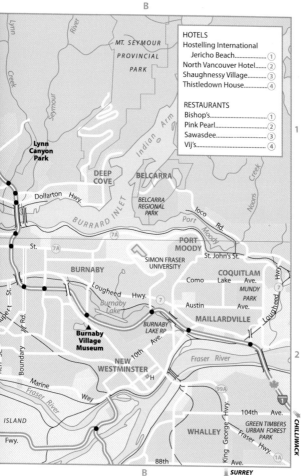

HOTELS

Hostelling International
  Jericho Beach.................. ①
North Vancouver Hotel....... ②
Shaughnessy Village............ ③
Thistledown House............... ④

RESTAURANTS

Bishop's.............................. ①
Pink Pearl........................... ②
Sawasdee............................ ③
Vij's.................................... ④

to Lynn Valley Rd. exit; turn right on Lynn Valley Rd. and right on Peters Rd. to the park. 604-981-3103. www.dnv.org/ecology. *Open year-round daily 7am; closing hours vary. Ecology Centre (604-990-3755) open Mon–Fri 10am–5pm, Sat–Sun and holidays noon–4pm; closed Dec 25–Jan 1. Suggested donation $2 per person or $5 per family.*

East of Capilano Canyon, along the North Shore, this 250ha/617acre regional park straddles the canyon of a swift and cold North Shore river, **the Lynn**. Trails lead along the canyon rim, through deep forest and into the gorge, where emerald swimming holes await hardy souls. Some 60m/197ft above the forest floor, a short suspension **bridge★** carries a trail across the canyon. The **Ecology Centre** features informative exhibits on the park's forests and its denizens.

Capilano River Regional Park

Access from Capilano Rd., just north of the Capilano suspension bridge; and at Cleveland Dam, north end of Capilano Rd. 604-224-5739. www.metrovancouver.org.

Encompassing the river's narrow gorge and its hillsides, this park has peaceful **hiking trails**, streamside spots for picnicking and contemplation, and scattered patches of old-growth forest. The lower entrance to the park leads to the **Capilano Salmon Hatchery**, where visitors can take a self-guided tour to learn about the life cycle of migrating salmon and steelhead. At the north end of the park, **Cleveland Dam** impounds a drinking-water reservoir; the top of the dam has excellent **views** of

the Lions, the two peaks for which Lions Gate is named.

EAST FRASER VALLEY

Originating in Canada's Rocky Mountains, the **Fraser River** is British Columbia's longest river. The narrow, 145km/90mi expanse of flat river bottom stretching south and east from Vancouver has long been the city's agricultural fringe—and now is its suburban growth area as well. The municipalities of Richmond, Burnaby, Delta, Surrey and New Westminster all have their own city centres, and their own attractions. But they are inarguably satellites to Vancouver, which connects to them via the two Lower Mainland freeways, Highway 99 south to the US border, and Highway 1 (the Trans-Canada Highway) east to Hope.
East of Surrey, development lessens, and the countryside reverts to farmland between Langley and Abbotsford, and on to Chilliwack. The latter community is famed for its **produce stands,** which in August and September offer huge bins of freshly picked Chilliwack corn.

Burnaby Village Museum★

14km/9mi east of Vancouver via Hastings St. E. east to Hwy. 1; take the Kensington Ave. exit and go south on Kensington Ave.; turn left on Canada Way. 6501 Deer Lake Ave., in Deer Lake Park, Burnaby. 604-293-6501. www.burnabyvillagemuseum.ca. Open annually for Spring Break (dates vary), May–Sept daily 11am–4:30pm, late Nov–mid-Dec daily

Burnaby Village Museum

© Burnaby Village Museum

noon–4:30pm, mid-Dec–early Jan noon–8pm. Closed Dec 24 and 25. Prices vary seasonally by program.

Cotton candy spins at a picture show, penny candy fills jars at the **general store**. The clank of a hammer on hot iron resounds from the **blacksmith shop**. There's a moving picture show, an apothecary and an **ice-cream parlour.** This extensive complex reflects life in the Lower Mainland circa the turn of the 19C. Most of the 30-odd restored buildings were moved here from elsewhere. Costumed interpreters on-site offer insights on daily life of a bygone era. The 1912 **carousel**★★ *(rides $2.30)* delights kids now as much as it did nearly a century ago.

Fort Langley National Historic Site★

56km/35mi southeast of Vancouver via Hwy. 1. Glover St. and Mavis Ave., in Langley. 604-513-4777. www.pc.gc.ca. Open year-round daily 10am–5pm. $7.80.

Opened as a Hudson's Bay Company trading post in 1827, this fort played a key role in the settlement of British Columbia for 50 years. Trappers and traders were the first to pass through; then, starting in 1860, gold rushers came here on their way to the Cariboo. British Columbia was declared a British crown colony at the post's **Big House** in 1858—an event still commemorated here today. Set on a cottonwood-shaded rise beside the Fraser River, the wooden-palisaded compound includes restored or reconstructed buildings. The **storehouse**, the only structure original to the site, has a fine **collection of furs** and

the trading goods once exchanged for them. Costumed interpreters play the part of carpenters, trappers, schoolmarms, coopers (barrel-makers) and blacksmiths.

Harrison Hot Springs★

129km/80mi east of Vancouver. Take Hwy. 1 on the south side of the Fraser River to the exit for Agassiz-Harrison (Exit 135) beyond Chilliwack; then Rte. 9 across the river to Kent and continue north on Rte. 9 for 6km/4mi.

This famed resort remains the nearest hot spring to Vancouver and a strong draw for weekend getaways. **Harrison Lake** stretches from here north into the forested vastness of the Coast Range. Set on the south end of the lake (the springs were discovered by boaters who noticed an upwelling of unusually warm water), the resort offers broad sandy beaches that are the site of a celebrated sandcastle competition each September. **Harrison Hot Springs Resort and Spa** *(100 Esplanade; 604-796-2244; www.harrisonresort.com)* draws hot mineral water from underground springs in the lake to fill its soaking pools. You'll also find lodging, dining and spa facilities here.

Hell's Gate Airtram★

52km/32mi north of Hope via Hwy. 1. 604-867-9277. www.hells gateairtram.com. Open mid-Apr–Thanksgiving Monday (second Mon in Oct) daily 10am–4pm. $21.

Fraser Canyon is 180m/600ft deep here, but the rushing river measures only 36m/120ft wide. Early explorer Simon Fraser named

Hell's Gate Airtram

© Hell's Gate Airtram

this terrifying narrows along the river that bears his name. He wrote in his journal: "We had to travel where no human being should venture—for surely we have encountered the gates of Hell." Once wider, the river was narrowed to its current width by railroad construction in the early 1900s. Through it roars twice as much water as at Niagara Falls. The airtram's gondola descends 152m/500ft from the highway above and crosses the chasm to a landing on the west side, offering a thrilling ride and great views of the narrows.

On the opposite side of the river is a small tourist village with souvenir shops. Visitors can hike down a steep road (.5km/.3mi) just south of the airtram parking lot to look at the narrow defile.

Hope★

150km/93mi east of Vancouver via Hwy. 1.

This erstwhile logging town occupies a small pocket along the Fraser River between the Cascade and Coast mountains, and is considered the farthest reach of the Lower Mainland. (Residents of the rest of interior BC refer to the notorious dichotomy in perspective between themselves and Vancouverites by declaring in jest that they live "beyond Hope.") The wildness and unpredictability of the region were well demonstrated by the **Hope Slide** of 1965, when an immense amount of rock from Johnson Peak *(18km/11mi east by Hwy. 3)* slid into the valley, filling up a lake. Chainsaw carving is big in these parts; a guide to the two dozen **sculptures** scattered around town is available at the **visitor centre** *(919 Water Ave.; 604-869-2021; www.hopebc.ca)*.

FRASER RIVER DELTA

At New Westminster, the Fraser River divides into two major arms, forming a classic fan-shaped delta estuary. Although the flatlands of the delta—its fine soils once were home to numerous farms—are now being converted to suburbs, the area's attractions still derive from its fishing and farming history, and its large population of waterfowl and migratory birds.

George C. Reifel Bird Sanctuary★

32km/20mi south of Vancouver via Hwy. 99 (Exit 28) and Hwy. 17. At Ladner, take Ladner Trunk Rd. west to River Rd. and cross the bridge onto Westham Island. Turn right on Robertson Rd. to the sanctuary. 604-946-6980. www.reifelbirdsanctuary.com. Open year-round daily 9am–4pm. $5. No pets allowed on premises.

Moored fishing boats in Steveston

©Volodymyr Kyrylyuk/Bigstockphoto.com

Birders take note: this stopover point on the Pacific flyway is one of the most important bird-watching locales in the Vancouver area—more than 260 species have been sighted. Encompassing 300ha/850 acres of wetlands and marsh in the Fraser River Estuary, the sanctuary lands were set aside in the 1960s by George H. Reifel. During **snow geese** migration *(Nov and Apr)*, as many as 30,000 of the white geese gather here, creating an unforgettable sight. Rare **tundra swans** have been spotted. Don't forget your binoculars.

Steveston Village★★

27km/17mi south of Vancouver via Hwy. 99 south to Steveston Hwy. (Exit 32); follow Steveston Hwy. west to Fourth Ave. and turn left. Visitor information 604-821-5474 or www.steveston.bc.ca.

Salt tang flavours the air. The creak of rigging and hulls on dock lofts along the shore. Mist rolls in off the water. You'll savour the atmosphere of a century-old fishing village in this historic complex. Spurred by the restoration of several of its historic sites, the village itself, with its numerous shops and cafes, has become a destination. Fishing isn't dead here; the marina still berths 1,000 boats, including commercial fishers who ply local waters.

Gulf of Georgia Cannery National Historic Site★★

12138 Fourth Ave., Steveston Village. 604-664-9009. www.pc.gc.ca. Open year-round daily 10am–5pm. $7.80.

The last major cannery on the Fraser River shut down for good in 1979 after almost a century packing salmon, halibut and herring. Now a museum, the complex features a model **canning line** and fascinating exhibits on the heyday of the salmon-packing industry.

EXCURSIONS

The area around Vancouver in British Columbia's southwest corner holds some of the most popular travel destinations in North America. Some, such as Victoria, are urban attractions. Others like Pacific Rim National Park and the Tofino area, rely on their natural wonders to draw visitors. Still others, like Whistler, combine both: spectacular natural features, outdoor recreation and top-notch civilized amenities. To fully appreciate them all would take months, but a one- or two-day side trip to any of them is eminently worthwhile.

VICTORIA★★★

On Vancouver Island. Access from Vancouver via ferry or air only (see Practical Information).

The British Colonial flair that has long characterized Victoria is as evident as ever, but savvy travellers look beyond **afternoon tea** and **horse-drawn carriages** to enjoy the city's beautiful **gardens**, multicultural flavour and outstanding natural setting. Facing the Strait of Juan de Fuca, the city is famous for the mild climate that has made it a **garden capital** and a popular retirement centre as well. Founded in 1843 as a Hudson's Bay Company outpost, and designated the colonial capital in 1862, Victoria was once the next stop on the British Empire circuit after Burma

Touring Tip

City centre is situated along **Government Street,** which is the main shopping area, and around the James Bay section of the harbour. Along the harbour **promenade★,** plaques honour clipper ships that once arrived from British Empire outposts. Nearby, shops and cafes border **Bastion Square.** Just north, Victoria's **Chinatown** begins at Herald Street.

(today's Myanmar) and Hong Kong, from which clipper ships called with tea and other Asian goods. Seat of the provincial government since 1868, Victoria is BC's second-largest metropolitan area, with a population of about 500,000.

Royal British Columbia Museum

©Royal BC Museum

MUST SEE

🦅 Royal British Columbia Museum ★★★

675 Belleville St. 250-356-7226 or 888-447-7977. www.royalbc museum.bc.ca. Open year-round daily 10am–5pm (until 10pm Fri–Sat). IMAX theatre daily 10am–8pm. Closed Jan 1 and Dec 25. $16; special exhibits may command a surcharge of $5.

You could easily spend a day at one of Canada's most-visited museums. The Royal BC focuses on the natural and human history of the province, and is most noted for its depiction of First Nations life. Here's an overview of the permanent exhibits.

First Peoples Gallery
The 🦅 **totems** on the first and third floors range from well-weathered historic pieces gathered at coastal villages in the 19C to stunning 20C works carved by artists such as **Bill Reid** (*see Museums*) and **Mungo Martin**. Faced with the graceful, geometric forms used to represent ravens, bears, eagles, whales and other icons of coastal Native life, the totems exude as much power in the museum halls as they did in seaside villages some 150 years ago. Two dozen **ceremonial masks**, representing every coastal Native carving style, are stunningly displayed in a dark case where each spotlit mask seems suspended in air. Audio and video presentations depict the ongoing struggle of BC's indigenous peoples to adapt to the modern world, including the restoration of the **potlatch tradition** (during which the masks are used by dancers) that was banned by

Thunderbird Park
Adjacent to the museum at Belleville and Douglas Sts. This park has yet more **totems★★**, together with a longhouse in which Native carvers demonstrate their craft during the summer.

British authorities in the late 19C. Stroll through the **longhouse** and peer into the **pit house** to gain an appreciation for the lifestyles of the Native American inhabitants.

Modern History Gallery
In this gallery, you can explore 200 years of history, beginning with the days of the European **fur trade** with First Nations inhabitants. Here you can walk the streets of a pioneer **Old Town**; then visit an herbalist shop in a mock **Chinatown**. Finally, clamber around a replica of the *Discovery*, the ship **George Vancouver** sailed into BC waters in the late 18C.

Natural History Gallery
Exceptional **dioramas** in this exhibit space illustrate the

©Royal BC Museum

Kwakwaka'wakw Masks, First Peoples Gallery

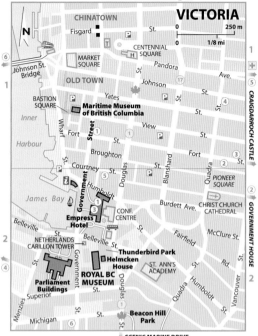

CENTRE OF THE UNIVERSE

VICTORIA

CHINATOWN

Fisgard St.

CENTENNIAL SQUARE

MARKET SQUARE

Pandora

OLD TOWN

Johnson St. Bridge

Johnson

Yates

BASTION SQUARE

Maritime Museum of British Columbia

Inner

Wharf Street

Fort

View

St.

Harbour

Broughton

Courtney St.

Government

Humboldt

James Bay

Burdett Ave.

Douglas

Blanshard

Quadra

PIONEER SQUARE

CHRIST CHURCH CATHEDRAL

Empress Hotel

CONF. CENTRE

Belleville

Belleville St.

Fairfield

McClure St.

NETHERLANDS CARILLON TOWER

Thunderbird Park

Helmcken House

ST. ANN'S ACADEMY

Humboldt

Vancouver

Parliament Buildings

ROYAL BC MUSEUM

Superior St.

Douglas St.

Quadra

Michigan St.

Beacon Hill Park

SCENIC MARINE DRIVE

CRAIGDARROCH CASTLE

GOVERNMENT HOUSE

0   250 m
0   1/8 mi

HOTELS		RESTAURANTS	
Bedford Regency	①	Bengal Lounge	①
Fairholme Manor	②	Blue Fox	②
The Fairmont Empress	③	Café Brio	③
Haterleigh Heritage Inn	④	Ming's	④
Magnolia Hotel & Spa	⑤	Paprika Bistro	⑤
Rosewood Victoria Inn	⑥	Spinnaker's Gastro Brewpub	⑥

province's varied **ecosystems**, from temperate rain forest to interior desert.

The museum is also a prominent stopping point for international exhibits, such as Egyptian antiquities, that sometimes visit no other North American venues. The lobby of the **museum's archives** now holds a rotating display of historic documents, diaries and photographs.

Helmcken House★

*675 Belleville St. 250-356-7226
www.royalbcmuseum.bc.ca.
Open for special events; call or
check online.*

This restored 1852 house, located behind the Royal BC Museum, was home to a physician to the Hudson's Bay Company at Fort Victoria. He and his wife raised their seven children here. Rooms

MUST SEE

are decorated in period furnishings brought around Cape Horn on clipper ships to Victoria.

Empress Hotel★★

721 Government St. 250-384-8111 or 866-540-4429. www.fairmont.com/empress.

Ah, the Empress, symbol of gentility. Designed by famed colonial architect Francis Rattenbury, this massive neo-Gothic granite landmark anchors Victoria's Inner Harbour. Since its 1908 opening, the Empress has epitomized the civility of the empire whose last days it witnessed. Over the years, this grande dame of hospitality has hosted royalty, celebrities, elite travellers and countless honeymooners. The hotel's public spaces include a vast **Edwardian lobby**; the glass-ceilinged Victorian **Palm Court**; the Crystal Ballroom; several clubby, dark-wood restaurants, lounges and sitting rooms; Willow Stream Spa; and the **Bengal Lounge**, whose colonial artifacts include tiger skins given to the hotel by the Thai royal family when they visited in the 1930s. Built by Canadian Pacific Railway as the westernmost

property in its continent-wide chain of château hotels, the Empress is now operated by the Fairmont group (*see Hotels*).

The Cougar Incident

As if to prove conclusively that no amount of civilizing can utterly tame Vancouver Island, one of the wildest of island creatures, a cougar, was discovered in the heart of Victorian urbanity—the Empress Hotel parking garage—in 1992. The garage gates were closed, wildlife officials called, and the cougar was tranquilized and returned to the wild. Victoria author Julie Lawson used the incident as the basis for a popular children's book, *In Like a Lion*—copies are, of course, available at the Empress news shop. Vancouver Island is considered by some wildlife experts to have the greatest density of mountain lions on earth.

Parliament Buildings★

501 Belleville St. 250-387-3046. www.leg.bc.ca. Open mid-May–Labour Day daily 9am–5pm. Rest of the year Mon–Fri 9am–5pm.

Intended to reflect the character, if not the actual majesty, of London's Parliament, this complex was

🍵 Tea at the Empress

Victorian matrons, no doubt smartly attired, were the first patrons when the Empress began its famous tea service back in 1908. Today both the dress code and the service have become less formal (no shorts though, please), but the atmosphere remains largely the same. Served in the hotel's elegant, high-ceilinged lobby, or in the Palm Court, afternoon tea is offered at five sittings a day. Traditional finger sandwiches, scones, crumpets, pastries, heavy cream and seasonal berry preserves are presented, along with the Empress' own proprietary tea blend. It's not cheap—figure up to $60 a person (varies by season). Reservations are essential: *250-389-2727.*

designed by **Francis Rattenbury** (*see sidebar below*), architect of the Empress Hotel. He blended (critics say he "mashed together") Victorian, Romanesque and Italianate design elements, including 33 copper domes, to create a complex that is one of Victoria's visual icons. The BC Legislature is in session here in winter and spring; **guided tours** (*45min*) explain the sometimes inexplicable workings of BC government, as well as the building's history. And what would a building of British heritage be without **statues**? An image of Queen Victoria stands out front, and Captain George Vancouver's likeness tops the highest dome.

Government Street★

Victoria's principal thoroughfare in Old Town is also its main shopping street, with venerable stores that are destinations in themselves. Here's a selection. Be sure to poke your head in at least one of them.

◆ **Rogers Chocolates** (*no. 913; 250-384-7021; www.rogers chocolates.com*) occupies a 1903 building with tile floors and oak display cases. The company began making its classic British-style truffles and candies in 1885. "Victoria creams" are Rogers' signature confection. They are definitely hard to resist.

◆ **Murchie's Teas** (*no. 1110; 250-383-3112; www.murchies.com*) dates its business back to colonial days, when clipper ships called from Hong Kong with tea bales on board. (Remember all the trouble that caused in Boston?) Like its counterpart branch in Vancouver, teas here range from everyday orange pekoe to $99-an-ounce handpicked blends that, believe it or not, are good enough to justify the cost.

◆ **Munro's Books** (*no. 1108; 250-382-2464; www.munrobooks.com*) sits next door to Murchie's in an elegant late-19C bank building, with high, pressed-tin ceilings. Munro's selection of BC books is superlative. Jim Munro, the founder and owner, was the husband of world-famous author, Alice Munro. The store celebrates its 50th anniversary in 2013.

◆ **Old Morris Tobacconist** (*no. 1116; 250-382-4811; www.oldmorris. com*) has a heady array of pipe tobaccos, which, signifying the store's British leanings, are stored in the humidor. The cigars are out in the open, and yes, Cuban cigars number among the selection.

Maritime Museum of British Columbia★

28 Bastion Square. 250-385-4222. www.mmbc.bc.ca. Open year-round daily 10am–5pm (Thu–Sat until 9pm). $12.

You'll recognize this building by the **lighthouse beacon** outside it.

Inner Harbour and Empress Hotel

©Leslie Forsberg/Michelin

Francis Rattenbury

Francis Mawson Rattenbury (1867–1935) lived a life as colourful as his famous designs are grandiose. Born in England, he achieved modest success as an architect until he moved to British Columbia, and wangled the commission to design Victoria's Parliament Buildings in the late 1890s. That got him hired by Canadian Pacific folks, who set him to work designing the Empress Hotel. Rattenbury cut quite a figure in BC society, until the revelation of an affair with Alma Pakenham, who was 30 years his junior, drove both from the New World back to the Old. There Rattenbury was murdered; Alma and her new lover were charged. He was sentenced to life in prison, and she committed suicide.

Housed in the old courthouse, the maritime museum presents an eclectic collection of maps, artifacts, charts and model ships that depicts the province's seafaring past. Two small boats—a traditional **dugout canoe** and a **ketch**—offer up-close evidence of the adventurous spirit of the early mariners.

Inner Harbour

Along Wharf St.

The heart of Victoria edges this lively, boat and floatplane-filled harbour, with the Empress Hotel directly ahead, the Parliament Buildings to one side, and Old Town to the other. Here, on a summer day, fresh breezes blow off the water, street musicians ply their craft on stone benches, hanging baskets of petunias and geraniums glisten in the sun, and you could almost swear it was the year 1900. **Tourism Victoria's** main visitor centre is located at the west end of the Inner Harbour (*812 Wharf St.; 250-953-2033 or 800-663-3883; www.tourismvictoria.com; open May–Sept daily 8:30am–8:30pm, rest of the year daily 9am–5pm; closed Dec 25*).

Chinatown

Bounded by Pandora Ave., Herald, Government and Store Sts.

Encompassing two city blocks, Victoria's Chinatown, though much smaller in scale than Vancouver's, has a lot of the same flavour—tea, herb and spice shops; stalls with exotic produce; Asian imports stores; and dim sum restaurants. The entrance to Chinatown is marked by the 1981 **Gate of Harmonious Interest★**, a lavishly figured, vividly coloured archway over Fisgard Street at Government. The adjoining **Fan Tan Alley**, just .9m/3ft wide at its narrowest, and reputedly Canada's narrowest alley, is a warren of small shops. Once this district harboured gambling and opium dens.

Silk Road Tea
1624 Government St. 250-388-6815. www.silkroadtea.com.
Get a whiff of this superlative tea and bath shop in Chinatown, which proffers bath salts and soaps containing exotic herbs and oils, such as fir and geranium.

⚓ Scenic Marine Drive★★

Begin at Thunderbird Park, Douglas and Belleville Sts.

This drive reveals Victoria's splendid setting on the **Strait of Juan de Fuca**, yielding views of the city's gardens, neighbourhoods and scenic vistas. Start at Thunderbird Park, and head south on Douglas Street, past Beacon Hill Park and a plaque noting the starting point of Highway 1, the Trans-Canada Highway. Turn left on Dallas Road, heading east along the water. At Finlayson and Cover Points, enjoy **panoramic views** of the strait, with the Olympic Mountains in Washington State in the distance.

Centre of the Universe★

5071 W. Saanich Rd. Travel north on Hwy. 17A to Little Saanich Mountain. 250-363-8262. www.nrc-cnrc.gc.ca/cu .Open year-round daily 3:30pm–11:15pm. $13.50.

In 1918, when it first went into service, this observatory's 1.6m/65in telescope was the largest in the world. No longer, of course, but it has one inestimable distinction today: visitors are allowed to actually turn the instrument themselves. On clear nights, vast celestial views abound; the nearby interpretive centre features intriguing displays about Canadian contributions to heavenly exploration.

Craigdarroch Castle★

1050 Joan Crescent. 250-592-5323. www.thecastle.ca. Open mid-Jun–Labour Day daily 9am–7pm, rest of year daily 10am–4:30pm. Closed Jan 1 and Dec 25–26. $13.75.

Scottish immigrant **Robert Dunsmuir** was BC's first tycoon, a coal baron who meant this castle to be the most grandiose home on North America's Pacific coast. The mansion was finished in the late 1890s but, in an irony of biblical proportions, Dunsmuir was never able to glory in his creation—he died before it was done. The four-storey sandstone, granite

---

An Empire of Antiques

Just as colonial civil servants wended their way to Victoria to retire, so did their bric-a-brac possessions. That was long ago, of course, but the tradition of selling antiques in this city has as much heritage as any of its Victorian buildings. Today almost all the finer antique stores are concentrated in a three-block stretch of Fort Street, from Blanshard Street uphill to Cook. Here you can find anything from rare Burmese tapestries to early rock 'n roll 45s (if you even remember what those are!), and the selection of silverware, crystal and crockery is exceptional. Here's a sampling of shops:

♦ **Romanoff & Company** *(837 Fort St.; 250-480-1543)* has thousands of pieces of exquisite china and dinnerware.

♦ **Wells Books** *(824 Fort St.; 250-360-2929)* carries countless rare volumes and specializes in nautical texts.

♦ **Antiquarian Print Room** *(840 Fort St.; 250-380-1343)* focuses on maps and prints from the Victorian era and earlier.

Craigdarroch Castle

©Bruce Davies/Craigdarroch Castle

Touring Tip

Butchart's popularity has its drawbacks: peak summer days can find more than 50 tour buses in the huge parking lot, and the crowded paths can dampen your experience somewhat. Garden managers do what they can to minimize the effects of crowding (smoking is forbidden, for instance), but it's best to arrive early, or visit in spring and fall. In summer however, a **fireworks display** lights up the sky on Saturday nights. For a small re-admission fee *($3.50)* you can return the following day, provided it's not a special events day, to spread your visit over two days. The on-site store sells a vast array of books devoted to gardening, botany and horticulture, as well as souvenirs and gift items. There is a restaurant on the premises.

and marble structure, complete with turrets and towers, shelters an opulent interior. Inside, meticulously hand-carved walls and intricate ceiling panelling greet visitors. Numerous ceiling-high **stained-glass panels** outshine all but the world's biggest cathedrals. The 87 steps of the massive oak stairway lead to a fourth-floor **ballroom**.

🌲 Butchart Gardens★★★

North of Victoria, in Brentwood Bay. Take Hwy. 17 to Keating Cross Rd. 250-652-4422 or 866-652-4422. www.butchartgardens.com. Open year-round daily 9am–dusk (opens at 1pm Dec 25). $29.60 mid-Jun–Sept; $24.75 Oct; $19.15 Nov; $24.50 Dec–Jan 6; $16.70 Jan 7–14; $22.40 Jan 15–Mar 20; $28.10 Mar 21–Jun 14.

When you see these spectacular gardens, you'll be hard-pressed to imagine that this site was once a gaping quarry. In 1904 Jennie Butchart had a vision for the operations. The 20ha/50 acres of gardens that resulted have achieved world fame for their splendour and variety. Still run by the Butchart family and headed by Jennie's great-granddaughter, the gardens are among Canada's most popular attractions.

Sunken Garden

The justly famed and oft-pictured heart of the old quarry is the **centrepiece garden**. Green lawns curve around carefully tended masses of bright annuals, perennials and bulbs. The displays change with the season, and even winter has its blooms.

Sunken Garden, Butchart Gardens

Courtesy of The Butchart Gardens

Ross Fountain

Within a rocky pool at the south end of the Sunken Garden, dramatic **water displays** feature changing patterns and, at night, an array of coloured lights.

Rose Garden

This popular plot holds a maze of bloom-covered arbors in peak season *(Jun–Sept)*, attracting rose lovers from around the world.

Japanese Garden

A secluded spot, the garden features exquisite lacquered **bridges** and wooden **teahouses**.

Italian Garden

This formal garden has **statuary** and a star-shaped **lily pond** surrounded by colourful plantings.

Fort Rodd Hill National Historic Site★★

603 Fort Rodd Hill Rd. 14km/9mi west of Victoria via Rtes. 1, 1A and Ocean Blvd. 250-478-5849.www. pc.gc.ca. Open mid-Feb–Oct daily 10am–5:30pm. Rest of the year daily 9am–4:30pm. Closed Dec 25. $4.

Set on 18ha/44 acres of land at the southwest corner of Esquimalt's harbour, this fort defended Victoria and the nearby Esquimalt naval base from 1878 until 1956. Today the ruins of three coastal artillery **gun batteries** remain to tell the tale. Wander through the guardhouses, barracks and magazines to get a feel for day-to-day life in the garrison long ago. Built in 1860, **Fisgard Lighthouse** was the first permanent light on the west coast of Canada; the house where the light's keeper once lived now contains exhibits and videos relating to the site. Here you'll also enjoy great **views★** of Juan de Fuca Strait and the Olympic Mountains. **Langley Centennial Museum** *(see Museums)* is located nearby.

◤PACIFIC RIM NATIONAL PARK RESERVE★★★

Take Hwy. 1 north from Victoria to Parksville, then take Hwy. 4 west, through Port Alberni to the park. 250-726-7721.www.pc.gc. Open daily year-round; park facilities closed mid-Oct–mid-Mar. $7.80.

Wave-tossed rocky headlands, lengthy sand beaches, old-growth spruce forests and an inland sound with untouched islands are some of the natural elements that make up this outstanding natural preserve. Hugging the west coast of Vancouver Island, the National Park includes three distinct units: Long Beach, Broken Group Islands and West Coast Trail. The park's **visitor centre** *(open mid-Mar–mid-Oct daily 9am–6pm; 250-726-4212)* is located just past the junction where Highway 4 turns north.

Long Beach★★

Stretching from just north of Ucluelet in the south, where Highway 4 turns north, northward to within 4.8km/3mi of Tofino, this area is the only part of the park reachable by a road. The namesake beach has almost 32km/20mi of shoreline, most of it open beach, with firm gray sand for strolling, offshore **sea stacks** to send waves crashing upward, and open expanses where the perfect curls of breaking waves draw dozens of **surfers** (Tofino is widely regarded as the surfing capital of Canada).

Radar Hill★★

About 29km/18mi north of the visitor centre, the 91m/300ft summit (highest on this stretch of coast) of this hill affords a 360-degree **panorama★★** of the ocean and the island behind it. The road ends in **Tofino★**, 33.5km/21mi northwest of the Ucluelet junction.

Broken Group Islands

The second unit, composed of more than 100 islands, is contained entirely within **Barkley Sound,** a small inland sound south of Ucluelet. It is one of the premier saltwater **kayaking** areas on earth. Permits are required to visit the

Salmon Fishing

Wild BC salmon is regarded as the most delicious (and healthy!) in the world. Rivers are abundant with salmon, and Vancouver Island has its share. **Big Bear Salmon Charters**, based in Ucluelet, offers salmon fishing tours for anyone interested in catching their own dinner. Guided tours and equipment, plus instruction, are provided. *www.bigbearsalmoncharters.com or 855-972-5666.*

islands; outfitting and transport to the sound are available in Ucluelet.

West Coast Trail

This legendary 75km/47mi wilderness trail traverses the coast between Bamfield and Port Renfrew. The arduous trek takes up to six days, the weather is notoriously temperamental, and reservations are necessary long in advance, as park officials limit yearly use to about 8,000 hikers.

Wickaninnish Centre

At end of Wick Rd., 8km/5mi north of the visitor centre. Open mid-Mar–mid-Oct daily 9am–6pm.

This interpretive facility explains the North Pacific ecosystem, including the life cycles of the **gray whales** that pass just offshore during their annual migration between Alaska and Mexico.

EXCURSIONS

NEAR THE PARK

♨ Hot Springs Cove★

North of Tofino; access by boat only. Charters leave Tofino year-round.

Few places anywhere on earth offer what this legendary **provincial park** does: an unparalleled sensory experience for bathers. The hot spring waters arise in a headland about 61m/200ft inland and spill down the rocky channel to the Pacific waters of Clayoquot Sound. You can sit in the **hot-water pools** and let the cold seawater wash over you as waves arrive. The view out over the ocean, the salt breeze, and the peaceful wilderness surroundings all combine to make one of the most memorable experiences of a lifetime. It's best to come here during the week in spring and fall, when crowds are low. Along the way, you might see whales, dolphins, sea lions and eagles. **Jamie's Whaling Station** is the leading tour operator in Tofino *(606 Campbell St.; 250-725-3919 or 800-667-9913; www.jamies.com).*

Tofino★

At the end of northern end of Hwy. 4, on Long Beach peninsula. www.tofino-bc.com.

This small harbour receives more than one million visitors in summer. Erstwhile logging and fishing capital, Tofino is popular as a **surfing centre**. The community's central role in the Clayoquot Sound logging furor has brought it a distinct countercultural flavour. You'll often see barefooted youths traipsing through town with hefty packs, just as you'll see pickup trucks piled high with fishing nets, and family vans with tourists. Tofino hardly attracted anyone in winter until the opening of Wickaninnish Inn *(see Hotels)* kicked off the storm-watching aspect of the coastal visitor industry. Whale-watching, surfing, national-park camping, upscale accommodations, commercial fishing, and holdover logging—it's a heady cultural mix in this little town, and that's part of its unique character.

Clayoquot Sound

Pocked by dozens of small islands, this vast body of in-shore saltwater northeast of Tofino has a fascinating modern cultural history. Settlement on the sound began with a Nootka band under the leadership of Chief Wickaninnish. In the 20C, plans to turn the sound's forests over to timber companies for clear-cutting provoked an international outcry that attracted protestors from around the world, especially Europe. At one point, demonstrators seized the bridge over the Kennedy River and blocked traffic on Highway 4 for two days. The uproar eventually forced the provincial government to back down, and all interested parties—timber companies, environmental activists, First Nations bands and local residents—hammered out an agreement that allows limited selective logging in the area, but not clear-cutting. The whole story, along with the delicate balance of life in the rain forest ecosystem, is told at the **Rainforest Interpretive Centre** in Tofino

MUST SEE

(451 Main St.; 250-725-2560, www.raincoasteducation.org).

♦ **Hanging Garden Tree** –
Along the main hiking path on Meares Island, just east of Tofino in Clayoquot Sound. Access by water taxi from Tofino.

Here's a natural sight that's worth a 20min hike: the 1,000-year-old Hanging Garden Tree. This much-photographed **Western red cedar** has been worn down over time into a bulky 30m/100ft vertical burl with numerous side-limbs and a base broad enough to anchor a suspension bridge. The cracks and shoulders along the trunk have accumulated debris, which decayed into soil and sprouted wind-blown seeds.

The Hanging Garden Tree became a visual symbol for the early 1990s campaign to protect the sound's forest from clear-cutting. The controversy has muted now, and the tree remains—a host to dozens of other growing things.

MORE MUST SEES ON VANCOUVER ISLAND

Cathedral Grove★★

Along Hwy. 4, about 16 km/10mi west of Parksville.
www.cathedralgrove.eu.

One of the last remaining **old-growth groves** on lower Vancouver Island was given to the province by lumber baron H.R. MacMillan. The Douglas firs in this magnificent grove approach 75m/250ft in height and 1,000 years in age. Short 🥾 **hiking trails** lead from the highway (which splits the grove) into the woods; an elevated walkway affords a good **view** of the

devastation caused by a fierce windstorm in the mid-1990s.

Cowichan Valley★

On Hwy. 1, about 80km/50mi north of Victoria.

As Highway 1 leaves Victoria, it climbs a steep grade called **Malahat Mountain**, atop which viewpoints afford sensational **views** of the Gulf Islands and San Juan Islands, with the US mainland's snowcapped Mount Baker in the distance. The road then descends to sea level, entering the valley of the **Cowichan River.** The name is an attempt to translate a Native word that means "warm land," a reflection of the area's benign climate. That climate has led to the development of a nascent **wine-growing district**. Most of the vineyards are fairly young, and viticulturists and winemakers are still learning the eccentricities of their climate (it may be warm, but it's not California). The area's road

Vignetti Zanatta

©Sean Fenzl

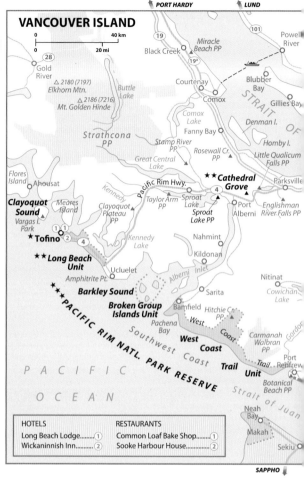

VANCOUVER ISLAND

0   40 km
0   20 mi

PORT HARDY

LUND

Powell River

Black Creek

Miracle Beach PP

Gold River

△ 2180 (7197) Elkhorn Mtn.

Buttle Lake

Courtenay

Comox

Blubber Bay

Gillies Bay

△ 2186 (7216) Mt. Golden Hinde

Comox Lake

STRAIT OF

Strathcona PP

Fanny Bay

Denman I.

Homby I.

Flores Island Ahousat

Stamp River PP

Rosewall Cr. PP

Little Qualicum Falls PP

Great Central Lake

Parksville

★★ Cathedral Grove

Pacific Rim Hwy.

Sproat Lake

Clayoquot Plateau PP

Taylor Arm PP

Port Alberni

Englishman River Falls PP

Clayoquot Sound

Meares Island

Sproat Lake PP

Vargas I. Park

Kennedy

Nahmint

★ Tofino

Kennedy Lake

Kildonan

Nitinat

★★ Long Beach Unit

Ucluelet

Alberni Inlet

Cowichan Lake

Amphitrite Pt.

★★★ Barkley Sound

Sarita

Broken Group Islands Unit

Bamfield

Hitchie Cr. PP

Carmanah Walbran PP

PACIFIC RIM NATL. PARK RESERVE

Pachena Bay

West Coast

Southwest Coast Trail

West Coast Trail Unit

Port Renfrew

P A C I F I C

Botanical Beach PP

O C E A N

Strait of Juan

Neah Bay

Makah

Sekiu

HOTELS	RESTAURANTS
Long Beach Lodge..........①	Common Loaf Bake Shop..........①
Wickaninnish Inn..........②	Sooke Harbour House..............②

SAPPHO

network is a farm-country maze, so it's best to phone for directions to the following wineries:

◆ **Vignetti Zanatta** *(5039 Marshall Rd., Duncan; 250-748-2338; www.zanatta.ca),* oldest in the district, it also has Vinoteca, a fine restaurant and wine bar in a heritage farmhouse *(open for lunch Wed–Sun).*

◆ **Cherry Point Vineyards** *(840 Cherry Point Rd., Cobble Hill; 250-743-1272; cherrypointestate wines.com)* has a tasting room that is open daily.

◆ **Blue Grouse Vineyards** *(4365 Blue Grouse Rd., Duncan; 250-743-3834; www.bluegrousevineyards.com)* is a family-run winery with a tasting room open four days a week.

MUST SEE

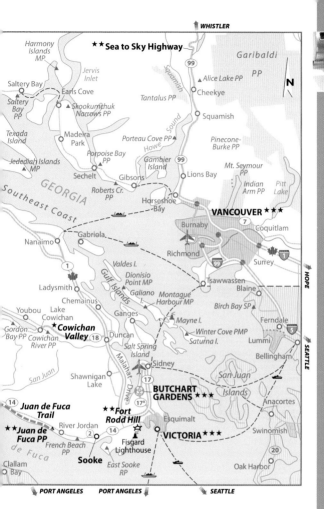

★★ **Sea to Sky Highway**

Harmony Islands MP

Garibaldi PP

Jervis Inlet

99

Saltery Bay

Earls Cove

▲ Alice Lake PP

Cheekye

Saltery Bay PP

Squamish Sound

Tantalus PP

Squamish

Texada Island

Skookumchuk Narrows PP

Madeira Park

Porteau Cove PP

Pinecone-Burke PP

Jedediah Islands MP

Porpoise Bay PP

Howe Sound

Gambier Island

99

Mt. Seymour PP

GEORGIA

Sechelt

Gibsons

Lions Bay

Indian Arm PP

Pitt Lake

Southeast Coast

Roberts Cr. PP

Horseshoe Bay

VANCOUVER ★★★

7

Burnaby

Coquitlam

Gabriola

Nanaimo

Richmond

99

Surrey

1

Valdes I.

Dionisio Point MP

Tsawwassen

Blaine

⬅ HOPE

1

Ladysmith

Galiano I.

Montague Harbour MP

Birch Bay SP

Chemainus

Gulf Islands

Ganges

Mayne I.

Ferndale

5

Youbou

Lake Cowichan

★ **Cowichan Valley**

Duncan

18

Winter Cove PMP

Saturna I.

Lummi

⬅ SEATTLE

Gordon Bay PP

Cowichan River PP

Salt Spring Island

Sidney

Bellingham

San Juan

Malahat Drive

Shawnigan Lake

17

BUTCHART GARDENS ★★★

San Juan Islands

Anacortes

14

Juan de Fuca Trail

17A

★★ **Fort Rodd Hill**

Esquimalt

Swinomish

20

★★ **Juan de Fuca PP**

River Jordan

2

14

Fisgard Lighthouse

VICTORIA ★★★

French Beach PP

de Fuca

Sooke

East Sooke RP

Oak Harbor

Clallam Bay

San Juan

◆ **Merridale Cidery** *(1230 Merridale Rd., Cobble Hill; 250-743-4293 or 1-800-998-9908; www. merridalecider.com)* is the leading West Coast orchard, with more than 4ha/10 acres planted with hundreds of apple trees—they pioneered hard-cider making in the West. Visitors are welcome year-round *(call for hours)*, but the best time to stop by is September and October, when daily pressings produce gallons upon gallons of highly flavoured juice.

Juan de Fuca Provincial Park

On Hwy. 14, west of Sooke. 250-391-2300. www.env.gov.bc.ca/

bcparks. Open year-round daily dawn–dusk.

This shoreline preserve runs from the Jordan River to Port Renfrew— in some places stretching less than half a kilometre (.25mi) inland from the beach. A multifaceted wonder, the park offers different levels of experience of the West Coast of Vancouver Island. Four access points allow **easy hikes** down to the shore, where Pacific breakers roll in on pebble-sand beaches; trails descend through old-growth Sitka spruce, massive trees with gnarled branches that may remind you of J.R.R. Tolkien's tree creatures, the "ents." **China Beach**, the first access, and **Botanical Beach**, the most distant *(2.5hrs from Victoria)* are the best beaches. At the latter, low tide reveals **tide pools** with anemones and nudibranchs, and starfish on the rocks.

Whistler★★★

Take Hwy. 1 in West Vancouver west to Horseshoe Bay, then follow Hwy. 99 north about 102km/63mi. Tourist information: Whistler Tourism Centre, 4010 Whistler Way; 604-938-2769 or 800-944-7853; www.tourismwhistler.com.

Less than 50 years old, Whistler today is one of the largest and most popular ski resorts in the world. Nonetheless it confines itself to a relatively compact developed area in a bowl-shaped valley deep within the Coast Range. The community has adopted a "bed cap" that limits residential and hospitality growth, since this year-round resort attracts visitors in all seasons.

If You Don't Ski

Fabulous restaurants, shops, spas and nightclubs await you 12 months a year. **Hiking**, biking, golf, canoeing, rafting, ballooning, fishing, climbing and horse riding fill the **summer**; in **winter**, go **ice skating**, dog-sledding, tubing, Nordic skiing and snowmobiling.

If You Do Ski

Two mountains that, combined, appear at the top of most ski resort ratings every year. No other area in North America has as great a **vertical drop**—1,609m/5,280ft. No other area has as long a season—skiing continues on the Blackcomb Glacier until August *(see sidebar below; www. whistlerblackcomb.com).* Whistler

Winter Olympics 2010

Whistler's founders in the early 1960s dreamed that one day the area would host a Winter Olympics. The fantasy came true in July 2003 when, in tandem with Vancouver, the 2010 winter games were awarded to the region. Among the area's virtues that appealed to the International Olympic committee is the fact that Whistler can handle an event of such global proportions with relatively modest preparation. Alpine events—downhill skiing, bobsledding, ski jumping—took place on Whistler and Blackcomb mountains. A bobsled and luge facility was built, but existing lifts and other facilities were sufficiently adequate. A Nordic ski centre was built in a nearby valley, adding to Whistler's overall appeal for years to come.

Skiing Whistler and Blackcomb

The season runs roughly November to April. Of the 37 lifts, 14 high-speed lifts can carry 52,000 skiers an hour to the top of Blackcomb Mountain and Whistler Mountain, two nearly identical peaks that face each other across a small valley. Annual snowfall averages 9m/30ft, and since the valley is clasped within the middle of the Coast Range 80km/50mi from Howe Sound, the snow is not as wet and heavy as at Northwest resorts directly facing the ocean. There are 200 trails, 12 bowls and three glaciers in 2,833ha/7,000 acres of ski-able terrain—the longest intermediate run stretches a luxurious 11km/7mi. The base is at 670.5m/2,200ft, and skiing tops out at about 2,286m/7,500ft on both mountains. One lift ticket covers both: *$98 in high season.*

advertises itself as a full-service resort; buy a ski/golf package to ski in the morning, and swing a golf club in the afternoon!

Whistler in Summer

In summer the area's setting and character draw large numbers of visitors for numerous outdoor activities.

♦ **Mountain Peeking** – Try the view from above. Take the **Whistler Gondola** *(open late Jun–late Sept daily 10am–4pm)* for a ride to the top *($30)*; you can even include a barbecue lunch at the mountaintop restaurant.

♦  **Biking** – Energetic visitors rent mountain bikes at the **Garbanzo Bike & Bean Shop** *(at the foot of the lift; 604-905-2076; www.whistlerbike.com)* and ride all the way down Whistler—the descent takes about three hours. Ride or bike down—you'll enjoy magnificent panoramas of numerous **Coast Range** peaks in every direction.

♦ **Canoeing and River Running** – **Whistler Outdoor Experience** *(www.whistleroutdoor.com)* rents equipment and provides guided tours for canoe trips on clear, cold **Green Lake** *(8km/5mi east*

of Whistler Village), and sponsors guided **kayak** and canoe trips down the **River of Golden Dreams**.

♦ **Golf – The Château Whistler Golf Club** *(604-938-2092; www.fairmontgolf.com/whistler)* was designed by Robert Trent Jones, Jr.; the 122m/400ft elevation gain along the course is softened by the GPS computers onboard the carts. **Nicklaus North** *(604-896-2224; www.golfbc.com/courses/furry_creek)*, designed by Jack Nicklaus, winds around Green Lake.

♦ **Fishing** – The streams and rivers around Whistler are rich with game fish like salmon, steelhead,

©Éric P. Lucas/Michelin

Dogsledding in Whistler area

Whale Watching off Vancouver Island

The whales that ply the inland and coastal waters of the Pacific Northwest are among North America's most beloved wild creatures. Thousands of sightseers board boats daily to head out in hopes of a glimpse of graceful black-and-white **orcas** slipping through the Georgia Strait, or the much bigger **gray whales** that migrate north and south along the Pacific coast between Alaska and Mexico. These cruises are among the most popular of visitor activities, but controversy accompanies them. Some conservation advocates (and some scientists) believe the unremitting presence of dozens of noisy boats interferes with the whales' daily lives, especially the orcas, who use sound waves to communicate and to locate prey. The three Puget Sound killer-whale pods, in particular, are in decline, though scientists debate the reasons. You can see whales from many shoreline points, such as those in Victoria's Oak Bay neighbourhood, though sightings cannot be guaranteed. Be sure the boat you board subscribes to the industry's code of ethics, which forbids chasing whales, and prescribes a minimum distance between boats and whales. For referrals to whale-watching companies that adhere to the code of ethics, contact **Victoria Tourism** (*250-953-2033 or 800-663-3883; www.tourismvictoria.com*). For information about whale-watching cruises from Vancouver, *see Outdoor Fun*.

trout and char, and opportunities abound for **backcountry fishing** adventures.

Whistler Flyfishing, long-established and with a great reputation, offers the complete package: an online store, two outfitting shops (one in Whistler and one in Squamish), guiding angling tours all year-round, and even a fly-fishing academy for those who want to learn how to do it right! *www.whistlerflyfishing.com or 888-822-3474.*

🛶 Okanagan Valley★★

From Vancouver, follow Hwy. 1 east, then take Hwy. 5 (the Coquihalla Hwy.) northeast, then take Hwy. 97C and Hwy. 97 east to Kelowna.

Clasped between towering highlands on either side, the Okanagan Valley runs north-south along its namesake lake and

river—a geographic happenstance that has resulted in a sun-rich climate perfect for growing **fruits and vegetables** (an industry that dates back to the mid-19C). The climate is also perfect for growing retirement communities. Modern development of subdivisions, golf courses and shopping centres has begun to threaten the viability of the region's longstanding agricultural community.

Okanagan Lake★★

Monsters unknown to science ply the 305m/1,000ft deep waters of this 121km/75mi-long spring-fed lake. So goes the legend, anyway; local officials have periodically offered a million-dollar reward to anyone who acquires incontrovertible proof that **Ogopogo** actually exists. So far, the closest claimant turned out to be a video of an extra-large beaver.

The lake is a geographic and recreational marvel—it never freezes; it has so far withstood the pollution of urban development; and it hardly ever varies much in depth, though its lower end has just a modest weir leading to its outflow. Boaters, canoeists, sailors, anglers, sailboarders and swimmers all enjoy its waters, as do countless waterfowl.

When you come down from the Okanagan Highlands on Highway 97C, the first sight of the sparkling blue lake is one of the more memorable vistas in BC. Ogopogo or no, this lake needs no exotic sea monster to embellish its wonder.

O'Keefe Ranch★★

Northwest of Vernon, on Hwy. 97, at the northern end of Okanagan Lake. 250-542-7868. www.okeeferanch. ca. Open May–Sept daily 10am– 5pm (Jul–Aug until 6pm). $12.

It's easy to see why Cornelius O'Keefe decided to stop here while driving cattle through the valley in the 1860s. The bunchgrass grew as high as a horse's belly, the breeze off the lake moderated the summer heat, and the setting still is as bucolic as ever. The ranch he built became one of the largest and most prosperous, with dozens of houses, shops, outbuildings and residents. Today this **BC Heritage Site** is the largest such historic ranch in Western Canada, with something for everyone.

The **general store** is stocked with goods from the turn of the 19C. The **O'Keefe Mansion** is an elegant late-Victorian house with cut glass, wood trim and front and back stairs (the latter were for noisy children).

The annual **Cowboy Festival** in late July is a real rodeo, with cowhands from nearby ranches competing for bragging rights.

Desert Interpretive Centre★

3km/2mi north of Osoyoos on Hwy. 87. 250-495-2470 or 877-899- 0897. www.desert.org. Open late Apr–mid-May and late Sept–Oct daily 10am–2pm. Late May–mid- Sept daily 9:30am–4:30pm. $7.

The southern interior of BC contains Canada's only **non-**

U-pick Farms

For decades BC families have hopped in their cars and driven to the Okanagan to pick their own. Fruits and vegetables are available at dozens of small farms throughout the valley—from Vernon in the north to Osoyoos in the south, though most are between Penticton (an hour south of Kelowna) and Oliver, a half hour farther south, along Highway 97. To find a U-pick farm, simply watch by the road for signs, and decide what you want. Peaches, apricots, nectarines, plums, pears, apples, strawberries, raspberries and blueberries are the major fruits; vegetables range from asparagus to zucchini, with tomatoes, corn and chilis especially popular. Prices are per pound, in the sack—the custom is that whatever you sample on-site is free. Many orchards offer picnic facilities for families who make a day trip of their fruit-picking journeys.

polar desert, and this preserve, established in the late 1990s, is designed to accomplish two aims: help protect the desert, and help people understand why it's important. Take a **guided tour** along the boardwalk through the sagebrush and sand landscape; along the way, naturalists explain the hardy creatures that thrive in this challenging ecosystem, such as endangered rattlesnakes and burrowing owls.

Keremeos Grist Mill★

Upper Bench Rd., just off Hwy. 3A, in Keremeos. 43km/27mi southwest of Penticton. 250-499-2888. www.keremeos.com/gristmill. Open May–Oct daily 9am–5pm.

First opened in 1877, this restored mill occupies a pleasant, pastoral spot in a beautiful upland valley along the **Similkameen River**. Tall cottonwoods line the streambanks, including the small freshet that turns the grindstone (yes, it's really stone) in the gristmill. Now a **BC Heritage Site**, the mill grinds flour just as it did more than a century ago. The gift shop sells the mill's flour, ground using grains from the Prairie provinces; the flour makes great pancakes and muffins.

Kelowna★

395km/245mi east of Vancouver via Hwy. 1 East to Hwy. 5 North to Hwy. 97C South.

The biggest city in the BC interior (metro area population is about 117,000) is a small, thriving metropolis whose agricultural past is being augmented by high-tech industry and tourism. The city's resorts rely on Okanagan Lake and the valley's dependably warm summers for their existence; the burgeoning **wine industry** has become a significant draw as well. The first European settler in the area was Father Charles Pandosy, an Oblate friar who established a mission along a creek in 1860. The remarkable houses and barns he built of hand-hewn cottonwoods—artfully joined by dovetail notching—still stand at **Pandosy Mission Provincial Heritage Site★** (*Benvoulin and Casorso Rds., east Kelowna; www.okanaganhistoricalsociety.org*). The rest of Kelowna's past is on view at a complex of museums downtown, chief among which describe the viticulture and orcharding industries.

Orchard Industry Museum
1304 Ellis St. 778-478-0347. www.kelownamuseum.ca. Open year-round Tue–Fri 10am–5pm, Sat 10am–4pm, holidays 11am–3pm. Here you'll see how the industry's development depended on transportation to get the fruit to market—by boat along the lake to a railhead, then on to Vancouver. One of the museum's most delightful aspects is the collection of Art Deco-style **fruit-box labels**.

Wine Museum
1304 Ellis St. 250-868-0441. www.kelownamuseum.ca. Open year-round Mon–Fri 10am–6pm, Sat 10am–5pm, Sun and holidays 11am–5pm. Closed Jan 1, Dec 25-26. Exhibits describe how pioneers had to overcome skepticism about the industry's potential this far north; Okanagan wines are for sale in the adjacent shop.

🍷 BC Wine Country

The warm summer climate and cool nights of the **Okanagan Valley** have proven ideal for growing wine grapes, and a happy accident (that at first seemed calamitous) led to the area's signature product. When a vineyard's grapes froze on the vines one fall, the winemaker let them thaw and fermented the juice into a sweet after-dinner drink called **ice wine**—BC ice wines now enjoy huge popularity in Asia, and many grape crops are deliberately left on the vines to freeze. BC now boasts more than 200 wineries. Dozens of these operate in the valley, mostly around Kelowna and in the arid valley south of Penticton. That city's **Wine Country Visitor Centre**, similar to the one in Napa, California, has winery pamphlets, touring maps, and a shop that sells an extensive selection of Okanagan wines *(553 Railway St., Penticton; 250-490-2006; www.pentictonwineinfo.com; open year-round daily 9am–6pm; extended hours in summer).*

Winning Wineries

◆ **Mission Hill Family Estate** – *1730 Mission Hill Rd., in West Kelowna. 250-768-7611. www.missionhillwinery.com. Tastings and tours daily.* Aiming to become one of the top wineries on earth (no small objective), this ambitious operation across the lake from Kelowna has invested millions of dollars in facilities—a large visitor centre, an outdoor performance amphitheatre, tasting rooms, dining rooms and extensive underground cellars. It's known for its chardonnay, merlot and ice wine.

Touring Tip

Looking for a place to stay overnight in Kelowna? The **Manteo Resort** *(3762 Lakeshore Rd.; 250-860-1031 or 800-445-5255; www.manteo.com)* offers swimming, sailing, tennis, volleyball and other recreation as well as a restaurant and guest rooms.

◆ **Quail's Gate Estate Winery** – *3303 Boucherie Rd., Kelowna. 250-769-4451 or 800-420-9463. www.quailsgate.com. Tastings and tours daily.* Located in a 130-year-old log home, Quail's Gate winery focuses on merlot, pinot noir and chardonnay.

◆ **Burrowing Owl Estate Winery** – *100 Burrowing Owl Pl., Oliver. Tours daily Apr–Dec. 250-498-0620 or 877-498-0620. www.bovwine.com.* This winery is noted for its intensely flavoured reds. At the winery's **Sonora Room** restaurant, you can taste how Burrowing Owl's wines complement fine regional cuisine.

◆ **Tinhorn Creek** – *537 Tinhorn Creek Rod., Oliver. 250-498-3743 or 888-484-6467. www.tinhorn.com. Self-guided tours and tastings daily 10am–5pm.* Nestled against the foothills on the west side of the valley, Tinhorn is famed for varietal reds such as merlot. Nearby Tinhorn Creek was the site of a 19C gold mine.

EXCURSIONS

FOR FUN

At one end of downtown Vancouver, horse-drawn carriages trundle visitors sedately through the peaceful woods of Stanley Park. At the other end, hockey players and pucks rocket across the ice in one of the most dynamic sports of all. The opportunities for fun in Vancouver are as diverse as the city itself—and they're available year-round.

GRANVILLE ISLAND★

On False Creek. Follow Granville St. south from downtown, then follow signs to loop back around under Granville bridge on W. 2nd Ave. Access also via ferry (see sidebar, opposite). 604-666-5784. www.granvilleisland.com.

A thrumming **industrial zone** in the period between the two World Wars, then a run-down collection of warehouses, Granville Island was transformed into an effervescent district of shops, stalls, galleries and cafes in the 1970s. Today it's a designated **heritage district** operated on behalf of the Government of Canada. It's a favourite of visitors and residents alike—especially the Public Market, where fresh foods abound, a dozen cultures mix, and the variety of smells, flavours, sights and sounds is a feast for the senses.

Included in the cosmopolitan mix is a still-humming cement plant that testifies to the island's industrial past.

The island fills 12ha/29 acres with attractions; the place to start is the **Granville Island information kiosk** *(Johnston and Cartwright Sts.; 604-666-5784)*. Maps are available to guide you around, and the bulletin board is a colourful menu of island goings-on.

Public Market★

Granville Island; for access, see sidebar. 604-666-6477. www.granvilleisland.com. Open year-round daily 9am–7pm. Closed Jan 1 and Dec 24–25.

A large, hangar-like building right along False Creek, the Public Market is the most-visited and best-loved facility on the island. Here you can wander

Granville Island Public Market

©Leslie Forsberg/Michelin

MUST DO

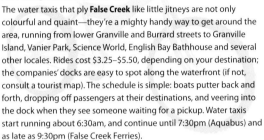

Getting to Granville Island

Aquabus *604-689-5858; www.theaquabus.com.* **False Creek Ferries:** *604-684-7781; www.granvilleislandferries.bc.ca.*

The water taxis that ply **False Creek** like little jitneys are not only colourful and quaint—they're a mighty handy way to get around the area, running from lower Granville and Burrard streets to Granville Island, Vanier Park, Science World, English Bay Bathhouse and several other locales. Rides cost $3.25–$5.50, depending on your destination; the companies' docks are easy to spot along the waterfront (if not, consult a tourist map). The schedule is simple: boats putter back and forth, dropping off passengers at their destinations, and veering into the dock when they see someone waiting for a pickup. Water taxis start running about 6:30am, and continue until 7:30pm (Aquabus) and as late as 9:30pm (False Creek Ferries).

among dozens of independent stalls whose offerings embrace a cosmically broad range: artisan cheese and bread, seafood, fresh BC fruits and vegetables, condiments, jams and preserves, handmade sausages, butcher-block meats, crafts, and artwork. It's impossible to leave without buying something.

Stalls that surround the two food courts offer a world of cuisines, including Russian, American, Chinese, Thai, Austrian and Greek. At **Stock Market** (*604-687-2433 www.thestockmarket.ca*), cooks brew up steaming pots of soup; ladled into a bowl with a hunk of bread, this combination makes a splendid cool-season lunch. Noodles in the salads at **Zara's Pasta Deli** (*604-683-2935 www. zarasdeli.com*) are made fresh every morning, and **Kaisereck Deli** (*604-685-8810*) piles hearty meats and cheeses onto thick, dense bread. If you need a beverage to complement your lunch, **Okanagan Wine Shop** (*604-684-3364*) boasts a large inventory of British Columbia vintages.

Must-Stop Shops

Apart from the market, the rest of the island is a gathering of tin-sided warehouses that hold galleries and shops. At **BC Wood Co-op** (*1592 Johnston St.; 604-966-3500*), artisans transform the province's wealth of timber into beautiful furnishings. **Eagle Spirit Gallery** (*1803 Maritime Mews; 604-801-5277; www.eaglespiritgallery. com*) has a small but stunning collection of First Nations masks.

Granville Island Brewing Company

1441 Cartwright St. 604-687-2739. www.gib.ca. Daily 10am–8pm.

This brewery was the first microbrewery in Canada. Though its major production facilities, having outgrown this site, have been moved to the suburbs, small batches are still brewed here, and tours and tastings are regular events. You can vote your opinion on the experimental brews.

FOR FUN

Pirates for a Day

For a day on the water, rent a motorboat from **Sewell's Marina at Horseshoe Bay** (6409 Bay St., West Vancouver; 604-921-3474; www.sewellsmarina.com; a 17ft 60HP for 6 people is $227 for 4hrs). The waters of Howe Sound are usually calm, so pack a picnic lunch and let the kids pretend they are pirates while exploring the many islands and coves. The view from the water lets you see the normally hidden luxury homes along the coastline near Lions Bay, including the one used as Baltair's house in the *Battlestar Galactica* television series.

VANCOUVER LOOKOUT★

At Harbour Centre Tower, 555 W. Hastings St. 604-689-0421. www.vancouverlookout.com. Open May–Oct daily 8:30am–10:30pm. Rest of the year daily 9am–9:30pm. $15.

Though the view from this tower-topping, circular **observation deck** is expansive—it's the highest point in Vancouver—the ride up is what many visitors remember most. The glass-enclosed elevator soars 167.5m/550ft up the outside of the building, so it's not a good choice for anyone with severe vertigo. Once you're up top, you have a 🔲 **360-degree panorama★★★** of the city, with handy signs that mark everything you see. Top of Vancouver, the restaurant atop the tower, is a unique and lofty spot in which to dine with an awesome view (*604-669-2220; www.topof vancouver.com*).

STANLEY PARK CARRIAGE TOURS

Near Stanley Park information kiosk, Stanley Park Dr. 604-681-5115. www.stanleyparktours. com. One-hour tours depart every 20min, mid-Mar–Oct daily 9:40am–5pm. $29.99 for the basic tour. For more information about Stanley Park, See Parks and Gardens.

The clip-clop of horseshoes is a much better background sound for a tour of the park than engine RPMs. This long-established company offers group tours in horse-drawn wagons, with narration to describe the sights along the way. More intimate tours in private horse-drawn carriages, known more commonly in Canada as a "caleche," are available by reservation. The company provides shuttle service to its starting points, so you don't have to fight the parking wars along the park's roads.

JUST FOR SPORT

Though Vancouver's NBA team has departed, the city's two remaining major-league sports franchises are quintessentially Canadian and receive heartfelt (culturally and fiscally) community support. Both the **Vancouver Canucks** NHL hockey team and the **BC Lions** CFL football team have made trips to their sport's championships— Vancouver's headiest sporting moment since 1994. Back then, the Canucks qualified for the Stanley Cup finals, but lost the final game in the 2011 season to the Boston Bruins, a defeat that resulted in street riots and hundreds of arrests. But a community miracle of sorts occurred in the aftermath. Vancouver residents took to the streets en masse with brooms and shovels and cleaned up the mess. That same year, the Lions provided some solace by winning the Grey Cup, the CFL title, the sixth time in 10 appearances when they have taken home the top prize.

Why not take in a game during the season? Individual tickets may be hard to come by, since these sports are so popular:

BC Lions quarterback, Travis Lulay
©Jeff Vinnick/BC Lions

◆ **Vancouver Canucks** – *Rogers Arena, between the Dunsmuir and Georgia St. viaducts. 604-899-4610. www.canucks.nhl.com. Tickets for a single game: $66–$345. Season: Oct–Jun.* One of North America's most popular professional sports, **hockey** is central to Canadian life—millions of Canadians have grown up playing pick-up games on frozen lakes and rinks in community arenas. Seats sell out for most of the Canucks' home games, which can be boisterous events.

◆ **BC Lions** – *BC Place Stadium, 777 Pacific Blvd. 604-661-3626. www. bclions.com. Tickets $29. Season: Jun–Oct.* Canadian **football** has three downs (as opposed to four in the States) and is played on a longer and wider field. Canadians believe it is a much more exciting game than American football.

◆ **Vancouver Canadians** play minor-league **baseball** at Nat Bailey Stadium. *Jun-Sept. 604-872-5232. www.canadiansbaseball.com.*

MOWtown

With more than $1 billion of activity and more than 200 productions per year, Vancouver ranks right up there with Los Angeles, San Francisco, New York City and Toronto as a leader in North American film and video production. Because so many TV movies and series are now produced here, the city has acquired the nickname, "MOWtown," for Movie of the Week.

Popular films shot in the Vancouver area include: *Carnal Knowledge* (1971); *Legends of the Fall* (1994); *X-Men* (2002); *First Blood* (1982); *Happy Gilmore* (1996); *X-2: X-Men United* (2003); *The Accused* (1988); *Double Jeopardy* (1999); *I, Robot* (2004); *Russia House* (1990); *Scooby-Doo* (2002); *X-Men: The Last Stand* (2006); *Twilight New Moon* (2010); *Mission Impossible 4* (2011); and *Twilight Breaking Dawn* (2011).

FOR FUN

OUTDOOR FUN

Snowcapped mountains, glistening blue water and serene forests beckon everywhere you look in and around Vancouver, so it's no surprise that opportunities for outdoor recreation are practically infinite. The list includes sailing, swimming, skating, biking, in-line skating, skiing, snowshoeing, kayaking and canoeing. The city is known as a place where you can ski, sail and golf all in the same day, and energetic souls have done exactly that. A more mellow (and rational) approach is to spread the adventures out a bit. By skiing one day, kayaking the next, biking around Stanley Park after that— there's no chance you'll run out of things to do.

HARBOUR CRUISES★

1 N. Denman St., in Coal Harbour. 604-688-7246 or 800-663-1500. www.boatcruises.com. $25–$70; $80 for dinner cruises. Call for schedule.

Spectacular as Vancouver is from almost any angle, the most sensational way to see the cityscape is from the water that encircles it. Harbour cruises are hour-long narrated tours of the harbour; luncheon cruises head up **Indian Arm**, the mountain-ringed fjord just northeast of Burrard Inlet; and sunset dinner cruises run from Burrard Inlet over to **English Bay**, and out into the **Georgia Strait** and back. Sunset Dinner cruises *(2.5hrs)* offer live music, plus a West-Coast themed menu. You won't easily forget the sight of Vancouver's skyscrapers backlit by the sun dropping over **Vancouver Island**; the perspective gained by being on the water adds greatly to your understanding of what is, after all, a maritime world capital.

IN THE SWIM

Yes, Vancouver has swimming weather—three good months of it, from early July to mid-September—and the city's two major **outdoor pools** draw throngs on sunny days.

⬧ **Pool at Second Beach** – *Stanley Park Dr.* 604-257-8371. *$5.36.*

Harbour Cruises, sunset cruise

©Harbour Cruises Ltd.

Located in the southwest part of Stanley Park, Second Beach pool once held unheated salt water. Now filled with heated fresh water and outfitted with slides for kids, the pool still enjoys fresh breezes off English Bay.

◆ **Kitsilano Pool** – *2305 Cornwall Ave. 604-731-0011. $5.36*. Directly across the bay, at the intersection of Arbutus and Cornwall streets, the famed Kitsilano pool is the largest **saltwater pool** in Canada—and it's even heated.

JUST BEACHY

Vancouver's 12.5km/11mi of **beaches** not only are scenic, they offer a distinct variety of things to do. Sorry, no dogs (there are dog-friendly sections) or alcohol allowed. Other restrictions include: no smoking, no kites, no ball-playing except in designated areas, no fires (BBQ pits are acceptable), and no inflatable water toys. Lifeguards are on duty Victoria Day to Labour Day daily 11:30am–9pm. For information, call 3-1-1, or from outside Vancouver, 604-873-8000. (*mid-May–mid-Sept; www. vancouver.ca/parks-recreation-culture/beaches*).

◆ **English Bay Beach★★** – *Beach Ave. at Denman St*. A great place to swim, kayak, picnic and **people-watch**.

◆ **Third Beach★** – *West side of Stanley Park*. One of Stanley Park's two beaches, Third Beach is popular with locals who come to swim and sunbathe.

◆ **Jericho Beach** – *West end of Point Grey Rd.* Go fly a kite, enjoy a sunset or fish off the pier here.

◆ **Kitsilano Beach** – *North end of Yew St. at the waterfront.* Kitsilano's neighbourhood beach and

volleyball courts are magnets for sun worshippers.

◆ **Wreck Beach** – If you're interested in an all-over tan, this beach is one of Canada's most popular **nude beaches** (*steps lead to beach near the intersection of N.W. Marine Dr. and University Blvd., west of UBC campus*).

Kayaking English Bay

Ecomarine Ocean Kayak Centre is located at 1668 Duranleau St. 604-689-7575 or 1-888-425-2925. www.ecomarine.com. Early Jun–Labour Day daily 10:30am–1pm and 2pm–4:30pm. $65 for 2hrs.

Sea lions and harbour seals pop their heads above water to inspect you. Lovers stroll by on the Stanley Park seawall, oblivious to your presence. The salt tang of the air clears your head, and the insistent tug of the tide competes with the gentle roll of the swells to pull you this way and that. **Ocean kayaking** is a sensory pleasure anywhere—in Vancouver, following the south Stanley Park shoreline, it's a wholly unexpected urban adventure. Ecomarine rents single and double kayaks ; if you don't venture out into the sea lanes, little experience is needed. **Third Beach** is the best destination, where you can haul out on the warm sand for a picnic lunch before you head back in.

GO FISH

If you thought that **salmon fishing** was verboten, you haven't heard the whole story. True, some species and runs of specific types of salmon are threatened—but others are thriving. In an average year, the **Fraser River** draws up

OUTDOOR FUN

Pacific Salmon

Born in freshwater streams and rivers, sometimes hundreds of miles from the sea, salmon migrate to the sea to mature. After two or more years growing in the ocean, they return to the stream of their birth to spawn and (usually) die. There are **five types** of Pacific salmon— chinook (king), coho (silver), sockeye (red), pink (humpy) and chum. **Steelhead** is a type of trout that also migrates to sea and returns to fresh water to spawn, sometimes more than once. Some salmon reach magnificent size, more than 22.6kg/50 pounds. Unfortunately, many races in lower BC and in the US face survival challenges, chiefly from overfishing and habitat destruction. The Vancouver Aquarium *(see For Kids)* in Stanly Park has created a salmon **spawning stream**, which runs a mere 91m/300ft from Coal Harbour up to the grounds of the aquarium. Fish first stocked here in the late 1990s have established active runs that return to spawn each October.

to 7 million salmon returning to spawn. Federal saltwater fisheries' managers monitor salmon stocks closely to set seasons and catch limits; opportunities remain for visitors to go salmon fishing. Many **charter operators** these days encourage their clients to practice **catch-and-release**, but you can also have your fish frozen and shipped home. Seasons vary among species, but there is some kind of fishing available all year. Most of Vancouver's charter fleet operates out of the marina at **Granville Island**. Rates vary widely ($75–$550/person), depending on the duration of the trip, number of people and distance travelled.

♦ In Vancouver, **Bites-on Salmon Charters** (877-688-2483; www. bites-on.com) offers trips that leave from downtown.

The Lower Mainland still has an active commercial fishery, too. Wander by the **False Creek Fishermen's Wharf** (*east end of W. 1st Ave., just west of Granville Island*) to see (and buy) the fresh catch of the day, which might range from crab and shrimp to salmon and octopus.

WATCHING WILDLIFE

The huge wilderness that surrounds Vancouver holds a healthy array of wild creatures, ranging from **tidepool anemones** to gargantuan whales. Almost all have been subjected to consumptive use in the past, but legal and social changes are shifting the most popular wildlife activity from harvesting it to watching it. BC has more than 450 species of birds (most are migratory), from the **Canada goose** and **Great Blue Heron** to ravens and gray jays.

You can see many wild animals— from squirrels to **harbour seals**—simply by strolling through **Stanley Park**, but the more exotic species are the subjects of guided trips that delight thousands of visitors every year. In BC, whale-, eagle- and bear-watching lead the list. The first two are accessible from Vancouver; bear-watching tours require

Humpback whale

overnight travel from Vancouver _(contact Tourism BC; see Practical Information)._

♦ 🐋 **Whales** – Despite the fact that over the centuries whalers have nearly harpooned them to extinction, more than 20,000 **gray whales** still ply the migration route between the Bering Sea and Mexico each spring and winter. Gray and **humpback whales** and **orcas** (the latter also known as killer whales)—three pods (family groups) of which inhabit Georgia Strait and Puget Sound—can be seen on day trips that depart from Vancouver. Most charter operators depart from Victoria _(see Excursions)_, but **Vancouver Whale Watch** _(604-274-9565; www.vancouverwhalewatch.com)_ runs shuttles from downtown Vancouver to its dock in Richmond. Daily departures _(Apr–Oct)_ utilize Zodiac-type vessels, and on all trips naturalists are onboard.

♦ 🦅 **Bald Eagles** – One of the largest concentrations of bald (American) eagles in North America returns every winter to the **Squamish River**, an hour north of Vancouver, to feed on a rare winter salmon run. As many as 3,700 eagles roost in the cottonwoods along the river. **Canadian Outback Adventures & Events** leads two-hour 🛶 **raft** float trips down the river to view the eagles. The mountain-rimmed valley makes a beautiful setting in which to see the birds _(late Nov–Feb Thu–Sun, departing 10am; 800-565-8735; www.canadianoutback.com; $100 fee includes transportation from downtown and Whistler hotels, a light lunch with hot chocolate and use of suitable clothing)._

Fast Facts about Whales

♦ Like all mammals, whales are warm-blooded: they breathe air, and maintain a constant body temperature.

♦ **Gray whales** _(Eschrichtius robustus)_ make the longest seasonal migration of any whales, travelling about 20,000km/12,500mi each year.

♦ **Orcas** _(Orcinus orca)_, or killer whales, are actually a type of dolphin.

♦ Bigger than any dinosaur, the **blue whale** _(Balaenoptera musculus)_ is the largest animal ever to inhabit the earth. A blue whale can grow up to 34m/110ft long and weigh as much as 180,000kg/174 tons.

OUTDOOR FUN

113

FOR KIDS

Sandy beaches, majestic forests, snowy mountains and hundreds of small parks and play areas—not to mention a world-class aquarium and several interactive museums—make Vancouver a superlatively kid-friendly place. Though the formal attractions for children are excellent, don't forget that a short walk along the shoreline seawall to look for seals will delight your little ones as well.

Stanley Park★★★ for Kids

Northwest end of downtown.
See Parks and Gardens.

Stanley Park is the undisputed capital for young fun in Vancouver. The park's pleasures can be as simple as stopping to watch squirrels play, or building sand castles at one of its **three beaches**. Star of Stanley Park, the Vancouver Aquarium is a facility that will entertain the entire family.

🐟 Vancouver Aquarium★★★

Southeast corner of Stanley Park, at Avison Way. 604-659-3474.

www.vanaqua.org. Open late Jun–Labour Day daily 9:30am–7pm. Rest of the year daily 9:30am–5pm. $21, children $13.

A day here is not just fun—it's good for the world we live in. The Vancouver Aquarium has become one of the leading conservation enterprises in North America. The beautiful and exotic sea creatures it introduces to thousands of awe-struck humans are almost all threatened in some way, and the aquarium works hard to help them survive and to help us understand what that entails.

Superbly athletic marine mammals entertain the hundreds of delighted spectators who ring the arena pool. **Sea otters** frolic with balls in their enclosures. Trainers step into tropical exhibits to toss food to the **crocodiles** (one of the most popular daily events here). But throughout, the emphasis is on explaining the habitat needs, daily lives and ecological significance of the animals to encourage support for conservation.

The aquarium's famed orcas are gone, having died of old age or been sent to other marine parks, and daily shows now draw audiences with **beluga whales**—an exotic species for which the aquarium is one of the world's leading advocacy and research institutions. And while the shows

Clownfish cove,
Vancouver Aquarium

©Hamid Attie/Vancouver Aquarium

are hugely entertaining, the "acts" are drawn from beluga real life: when one of the whales pokes its head above the surface to spout water all over a trainer (kids take great delight in this), it represents a behaviour belugas use to dislodge food from the floor of their home waters in the Arctic.

Encounters with Fish and Other Creatures

Check schedules for feedings and show times when you buy your ticket.

◆ **Graham Amazon Gallery** — This indoor wing has caimans, crocodiles, anacondas, **piranhas** and the world's largest freshwater fish, a type of **gar** that grows to 3.6m/12ft in length. Don't miss the daily crocodile feedings.

◆ **Pacific Canada** — This large pavilion depicts the rich and colourful marine environment along the British Columbia coast, down to the surging tides that wash and nurture orange sunflower **starfish**, chartreuse **sea anemones**, and delicate cream-coloured **nudibranchs**.

◆ **Canada's Arctic** — Exploring the vast, dramatic water wilderness that is home to belugas and their northern aquatic neighbours, this exhibit showcases the extreme changes endured by marine life in the remote Far North.

◆ **Penguin Point** — Enjoy learning about these dapperly dressed, diverse birds as they waddle and swim about their special space, a replica of their natural **South African** habitat; it's possible to get fairly up-close and friendly with these cute, unusual birds.

Just for Kids

Ever wanted to spend the night with a shark? You can, in a manner of speaking, during the Vancouver Aquarium's **sleepovers**, when kids get to spend the night in sleeping bags among the galleries. Or have a "beluga encounter" and go behind the scenes to feed these charming creatures, experience their unique communication style, and even pat their tongues. At **Clownfish Cove** play area, tots can dress up as their favourite sea creature.

🚂 Miniature Railway and Children's Farmyard

West of Vancouver Aquarium. 604-257-8531. www.city. vancouver.bc.ca/parks/parks/ stanley. Open Jun–Sept daily 10:30am–5pm. Mar–May weekends and holidays 11am– 4pm. $5.50, children $2.75.

In 1886, Canadian Pacific locomotive No. 374 pulled into the Vancouver rail yards, completing the first train transit of Canada. The engine pulling the Stanley Park miniature train is an exact replica of Engine 374, a fact that means more to the adults than to the kids they accompany on the train. Children just enjoy the 15-minute ride through the towering cedars and firs along the small rise in the park.

In the adjacent 🚂 **farmyard**, kids can pet the tamer animals among the sheep, goats, pigs, cows, chickens, ducks—and one llama.

FOR KIDS

115

Travel by Trolley

The **Vancouver Trolley Company** *(604-801-5515 or 888-451-5581; www.vancouvertrolley.com)* offers tours and "hop-on, hop-off" city explorations year-round, including a Stanley Park Shuttle service. Trips on the red-painted cable cars can be day-long or point-to-point. Family **Goose Tours** are popular. The trolleys also operate in and around Victoria. *Sample 1day fare $38; Stanley Park Shuttle $8.93.*

BC Sports Hall of Fame★

777 Pacific Blvd., in BC Place Stadium. 604-687-5520. www.bcsportshalloffame.com. Open daily 10am–5pm. $15, children over 5 years $12.

Sports in BC go way back to the **war-canoe races** First Nations residents held two centuries ago. Packed exhibit galleries in this comprehensive museum trace the **snowshoe races** prospectors held for entertainment to the 1998 Olympics victory by Whistler resident Ross Rebagliati, who won the first **snowboard** gold medal ever. Kids wandering these halls peer up at sports legends past and present, in **curling** to **lacrosse**. Check out the **Hall of Champions** or the **Aboriginal Sport Gallery** that pays homage to the sports culture of BC First Nations peoples. New to the complex is a tribute to the Vancouver 2010 Olympics, including the opening ceremonies, awarding of medals and a replica of Roberto Luongo's goalie mask.

H.R. MacMillan Space Centre★

1100 Chestnut St., in Vanier Park. 604-738-7827. www.spacecentre.ca. Open year-round Sat and holidays 10am–5pm, Sun noon–5pm, Mon–Fri 10am–3pm; Sat astronomy 7:30pm–9pm; observatory opens 8pm. Closed Dec 25. $15, children $10.75 (eve $10.75); observatory by donation.

Located next to the Vancouver Museum, this facility crams a lot into a small space. Exhibits explain the basics of planetary orbits, the nature of galaxies and the history of human space exploration. A special section delineates Canadian contributions to the latter. Highlights are a **motion simulator**, which takes a virtual trip to Mars, the moon, or some other extraterrestrial locale; and

Granville Island Children's Market

Granville Island. Follow Granville St. south from downtown, then follow signs to loop back around under Granville bridge on W. 2nd Ave. Access also via ferry (see For Fun). 604-689-8477. www.kidsmarket.ca. Open year-round daily 10am–6pm.
"Daddy, may I have that?" Be prepared to hear that plea dozens of times at this aggregation of stores at the entrance to Granville Island. The multicoloured building holds 30 shops selling everything from model trains to games to dolls, in greater quantity and variety than you're likely to find anywhere else in town. The shops emphasize items handmade by local artisans.

Vancouver International Children's Festival

Vanier Park, late May. 604-708-5655. www.childrensfestival.ca.

This old-fashioned fair delights kids as much today as it did when it began 32 years ago. Tents and playgrounds are set up in the park south of False Creek for the Tuesday to Sunday affair, designed to entertain entire families. Mimes, jugglers, clowns and singers stroll the grounds; **puppet shows** and children's plays take place on the various stages. Cotton candy, hot dogs, lemonade, a **petting zoo**, stilt-walkers, sack races—there's something for everyone at the world's biggest children's festival. *Entrance fee $6; shows package $18.*

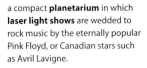

a compact **planetarium** in which **laser light shows** are wedded to rock music by the eternally popular Pink Floyd, or Canadian stars such as Avril Lavigne.

Maplewood Farm

405 Seymour River Pl., North Vancouver. 604-929-5610. www.maplewoodfarm.bc.ca. Open May–mid-Sept daily 10am–4pm. Rest of year Tue–Sun 10am–4pm. Closed Dec 25. $7.25, children $4.25.

Why do pigs wallow in the mud, and goats butt heads? You'll learn the answer to these questions and more at this once-thriving dairy farm, the last surviving agricultural enterprise on the North Shore when the regional Parks Board took it over to save it from development. Maplewood occupies a pastoral, tree-shaded spot along a creek, and it's hard to tell who's happier within its bounds—the 200 domestic animals and birds that live there, or the hundreds of kids who visit on sunny days. The ponies, goats, sheep, cows, ducks, geese and squealing pigs here are all well used to the intense attention children pay them.

Science World BC

1455 Quebec St. 604-443-7440. www.scienceworld.ca. Open Jun–Sept daily 10am–6pm. Rest of the year Tue–Fri 10am–4pm, Sat, Sun and holidays 10am–6pm. $23.50, children $6.75 . Separate fee for the Omnimax theatre.

This spherical **geodesic dome** perched at the end of False Creek may be the last structure remaining from Expo '86. Today what is affectionately known as the "golf ball" houses an **Omnimax theatre** as well as an astounding number of **interactive exhibits** and games that appeal to both adults and children. Geology, physics, electronics, biology, marine studies, zoology, physiology—hardly any scientific discipline is overlooked. For starters, visitors use synthesizers to make music; create square bubbles; generate plasma and electrical charges; and watch waves sweep the ocean floor.

Touring Tip

The fun way to get to Science World is on the **Aquabus**, the colourful little tubs that ply False Creek (*see For Fun*).

FOR KIDS

117

PERFORMING ARTS

Sure, Vancouver is a centre for the film and broadcast industry, but it's also a breeding ground for Canadian music. Stars who have begun or grown their careers here include actor Michael J. Fox, singers Diana Krall, Bryan Adams and Sarah McLachlan, and famed classical pianist Jon Kimura Parker. Symphony, opera, drama and dance alone will provide culture vultures with plenty of performances to keep them clapping in Vancouver.

Orpheum Theatre★

601 Smithe St. 604-665-3035. www.vancouver.ca/parks-recreation-culture/the-orpheum.aspx.

Designated a National Historic Site in 1979, the Orpheum is a one-of-a-kind arts palace from the era when the sky was the limit for theatre design. Opened in 1927, the 2,800-seat hall was once the largest theatre in Canada. Interior arches, columns and moldings of travertine, marble, stone and plaster were designed in Spanish Baroque style by Scottish architect Marcus Priteca. Converted to a movie theatre, it was scheduled to be divided up until community pressure in the mid-1970s spurred the city to buy the building and renovate it for use by the symphony.

Today the theatre is once again a glittering performance venue with few equals, hosting contemporary and classical musical performances that range from Steve Winwood to Jesse Cook. The original **pipe organ** still plays in half a dozen symphony concerts each year.

Arts Club Theatre

Granville Island, 1585 Johnston St. 604-687-1644. www.artsclub.com.

This busy and successful nonprofit theatre company is the one from which Michael J. Fox embarked on his TV and film career. It now mounts productions on three stages—two on Granville Island and one at the **Stanley Stage** (*see p 119*). The company's offerings range from avant-garde drama to classic musical comedy, with occasional original productions.

Orpheum Theatre

©Vancouver Symphony

MUST DO

Centre in Vancouver for Performing Arts

777 Homer St. 604-602-0616. www.centreinvancouver.com.

Once known as the Ford Centre, this striking building across from Library Square was designed by renowned architect **Moshe Safdie**. The conical glass tower over the entrance is one of those love-it-or-hate-it designs that modern architecture seems to relish. The centre is Vancouver's venue for touring **Broadway musicals** such as *42nd Street* and *Fosse*.

⚓ Queen Elizabeth Theatre

649 Cambie St., Hamilton and Dunsmuir Sts. 604-665-3050. www.vancouver.ca/parks-recreation-culture/queen-elizabeth-theatre.

Home to the city's opera company as well as its principal ballet troupe, this 2,800-seat theatre boasts a 70ft-wide proscenium arch stage. The **Vancouver Opera Company** (604-683-0222; www.vancouveropera.ca) offers four or five productions a year here, ranging from standard—Mozart, Puccini, Verdi—to original productions that tend toward the avant-garde. People still talk about a notorious production of Strauss'

Salome, in the mid-1990s, that was directed by Canadian filmmaker Atom Egoyan. **Ballet British Columbia** also struts its stuff at the "Queen-E," as it's called (604-732-5003; www.balletbc.com).

Stanley Industrial Alliance Stage

2750 Granville St. 604-687-1644. www.artsclub.com.

A massive community fund-raising project enabled the Arts Club Theatre company to take over this historic Art Deco building in 1998. Restored to their 1930s grandeur, the theatre's friezes, sconces and chandeliers glisten anew. Productions here tend to be revues, musicals and classic Broadway plays.

Vancouver Symphony

833 Seymour St. 604-876-3434 or 604-684-9100. www.vancouversymphony.ca.

While it regularly presents classic works by Beethoven, Brahms, Tchaikovsky and Mahler, the Vancouver Symphony frequently performs and occasionally commissions works by **Western Canada** composers during its year-long season; these pieces often incorporate elements of First

Tickets Tonight

Tickets for many musical and theatrical performances can be had for half price on the day of the show at **Tickets Tonight**, in the main Tourism Vancouver Visitor Centre *(Plaza Level, 200 Burrard St.; 604-684-2787; www.ticketstonight.ca)*. The **Alliance for Arts & Culture** is a clearinghouse for 350 performance arts of all kinds in Vancouver; it maintains a comprehensive schedule of events at its office at 938 Howe Street *(604-681-3535; www.allianceforarts.com)*.

PERFORMING ARTS

Nations music. Local musicians are featured, too, including members of the prodigious Parker clan, whose three sons are all established pianists. The symphony shares the Orpheum Theatre *(see p 118)* with other local and national touring companies.

More Musts for Performing Arts

Chan Centre for the Performing Arts – *6265 Crescent Rd., University of British Columbia campus. 604-822-9197. www.chancentre.com.* This sparkling facility at UBC is an elegant mid-size performance hall that welcomes national stars to its three stages.

Dal Richards Orchestra – *604-681-6060. www.dalrichards.com.* Western Canada's leading practitioners of big band and swing music make regular appearances throughout the Lower Mainland. Richards has been feature entertainer on special Holland America Lines' Alaska cruises, departing from Vancouver.

The Dance Centre – *604-606-6400. www.thedancecentre.ca.* Vancouver is a hotbed for modern and ethnic dance—especially Chinese, Japanese and Indian—and this clearinghouse organization maintains a schedule of performances at various venues.

Firehall Arts Centre – *280 E. Cordova St. 604-689-0926. www.firehallartscentre.ca.* Firehall hosts avant-garde drama and performance art, both local and touring, on the east side of downtown.

Vancouver East Cultural Centre – *1895 Venables St. 604-251-1363. www.vecc.bc.ca.* Live music and theatre hold the stage at this unusual historic venue, the renovated 1909 Grandview Methodist Church.

Vancouver TheatreSports League – *1601 Johnston St., Granville Island. 604-738-7013. www.vtsl.com.* This legendary troupe focuses on impromptu comedy and audience-participation events—giving an astounding 260 performances a year at the Improv Centre.

Festive Indeed

If you like festivals, you've come to the right place. Vancouver shows its dedication to the arts through a stellar, year-long lineup of festivals devoted to performance and cultural arts. Check the alternative weekly newspaper *Georgia Straight (www.straight.com)* or visit www.vancouverfestivals.info to see what's happening when you're in town.

MusicFest Vancouver

Various locations. 604-688-1152. www.musicfestvancouver.ca. Music of every description, from chamber to jazz, rings in 50 concerts during this citywide fest in early August.

Celebration of Light

English Bay. www.honda celebrationoflight.com. What's unique about Vancouver's annual two- to four-night showcase *(late Jul–early Aug)* is that the fireworks shower over English Bay to intensify the visual experience. The display is keyed to music, and fireworks artists from three countries compete against each other for first prize. It's free, too; the best seats are along English Bay Beach (the very best seats are at the reserved-seating barbecue at English Bay Bathhouse), but the show is visible from Kitsilano and the lower end of False Creek as well. If you want to be up close, arrive in late afternoon—thousands of people jockey for position.

Vancouver Folk Music Festival
Jericho Beach. 604-602-9798. www.thefestival.bc.ca. Folk artists from around North America perform dozens of different musical styles, from Tejano to French-Canadian, to Jericho Beach, in mid-July.

Vancouver Fringe Festival
Various locations. 604-257-0350. www.vancouverfringe.com. Fringe is perfect for a city whose political and cultural climate is Canada's most progressive. At this two-week festival in mid-September, you'll see performance art, impromptu groups, radical drama and multimedia presentations.

Vancouver International Comedy Festival
Granville Island. www.comedyfest. com. Jokes about rain are a mainstay at this event, especially since it's held in February, a notoriously wet time of year, although temperatures are beginning to climb.

Vancouver International Film Festival
Various locations. 604-683-3456. www.viff.org. The stars come out between late September and mid-October for this annual affair. Though it focuses somewhat on Canadian cinema, 300 films from 50 countries are included.

Vancouver International Jazz Festival
Various locations. 604-872-5200. www.coastaljazz.ca. This annual two-week affair at the end of June draws stars from around the world. More than a dozen venues participate, from intimate nightclubs to mid-size performance halls. Don't miss the two-day street festival in Gastown and Yaletown.

SHOPPING

Vancouver's remarkable cultural diversity—with its European, Asian and Native heritages—makes shopping here a treat. Here you'll find items not available in most other North American cities, including traditional First Nations mask art and nontraditional chocolate truffles shaped to look like First Nations art. Asian foodstuffs and furnishings in Chinatown complement European antiques along Main Street. Many American visitors flock to the city's tobacconists for Cuban cigars, forbidden in the States.

Robson Street★★

Once known as "Robsonstrasse" to reflect the street's erstwhile German character, this thoroughfare leading from downtown to the West End has transformed itself into a cosmopolitan district with ethnic flair. It is particularly popular with Asian teens, whose main objective for flying across the Pacific is to stroll Robson. (Yes, really.) On the blocks of Robson between Hornby and Denman streets, you can wear out your wallet buying everything from high fashion to yoga togs. When you're ready for a break, Robson is a prime place to 🔍 **people-watch**. Grab a seat at an outdoor cafe and check out the leather-clad bikers sipping lattés at Starbucks; purple-haired counterculture advocates heading for a demonstration at the Vancouver Art Gallery; Japanese schoolgirls walking hand-in-hand from boutique to boutique; and smartly clad office workers scurrying back from lunch. It's a parade you won't soon forget.

Robson Street Sampler

◆ **La Casa del Habano** (no. 980; 604-609-0511; www.havanahouse.com) offers a wide, if pricey, selection of 🔍 **Cuban cigars**.

◆ **Lush** (no. 1020; 604-687-5874; www.lush.ca) is a British soap and cosmetics maker whose delectable aromas drift out onto the street.

◆ **La Vie en Rose** (no. 1009; 604-684-5600; www.lavieenrose.ca) purveys fine European lingerie.

Lush

©LUSH Cosmetics

Gear for the Great Outdoors

The east end of the Broadway district is fast becoming a mecca for all manner of outdoor and recreational supplies. **Mountain Equipment Co-op** *(130 W. Broadway; 604-872-7858; www.mec.ca)*, a home-grown Vancouver institution that resembles its American counterpart REI, carries high-quality sporting gear of every description. Store personnel here also have a priceless inventory of information; ask them if you want to know something about outdoor recreation in Western Canada. On the other side of the street, **Altus Mountain Gear** has whatever you need for a Rocky Mountains-climbing expedition *(137 W. Broadway; 604-876-5255)*.

◆ **Roots Canada** *(no. 1001; 604-683-4305; www.roots.com)* is a branch of the clothing company that achieved world renown with its popularity at the Salt Lake Winter Olympics in 2002.

Antiques Row

South Main St., between 16th and 25th Ave.

The usual selection of furniture, crockery and jewellery is here, with a tilt toward British Colonial leftovers, and a new emphasis on Retro and Vintage from the 1950s and 60s. **Second Time Around**, which carries both eras and a lot in between, is located at 4428 Main Street and has twice been voted the number one antiques shop in Vancouver *(604-879-2313, www.secondtimearound.com)*.

The Bay

674 Granville St. 604-681-6211. www.thebay.com.

Yes, this retailer is the corporate descendant of the Hudson's Bay Company, whose traders established most of the first European outposts in Canada. Housed in a massive Beaux-Arts building downtown, the Bay has morphed into a mainstream department store. But you can still get **Hudson's Bay blankets**, just as trappers and traders did 150 years ago—you'd have trouble bartering for them with beaver skins, though.

Lonsdale Quay

On the North Shore of Burrard Inlet. 604-985-6261. www.lonsdale quay.com. Open year-round daily 9:30am–6:30pm (Fri until 9pm; restaurants open later).

Aside from the array of farm-fresh produce and 90 shops and cafes that await shoppers here, the best part about Lonsdale Quay is getting there. Take the **Seabus** ferry, which docks right at the quay and provides dandy views of the North Shore Mountains and downtown Vancouver en route.

Sinclair Centre

757 W. Hastings St., at Granville St. 604-659-1009. www.sinclair centre.com. See Landmarks.

Four historic buildings downtown are now linked under one glass roof as an attractive retail complex featuring **designer boutiques**.

Gastown Standouts

For anyone who likes classical and world music—that's all that's sold here—**Sikora's Classical Records** *(432 West Hastings St.; 604-685-0625 or 866-685-0625; www.sikorasclassical.com)* is a treasure trove, with more than 10,000 titles. At  **McLeod's Books** *(455 W. Pender St; 604-681-7654)* tables and shelves are piled high with used volumes spanning an array of subjects and authors far beyond the ken of modern chain outlets. Look here for the best in antiquarian books, many of those about Canadian history.

Shop Neighbourhoods

◆ **Chinatown★★** – *Bounded by Keefer, Abbott, Hastings and Gore Sts. See Neighbourhoods.*

◆ **Gastown★** – *Water St. between Carrall and Richard Sts. See Historic Sites.* Though Gastown is home to an array of T-shirt and tacky **souvenir** shops, chiefly along Water Street (how many little cans of maple syrup from Quebec do you need?), the adjoining streets have some more interesting retail outlets, like Westernwear stores, curio shops, home furnishings, and economical Native artwork.

◆ **Yaletown★** – *Bounded by Davie, Homer, Nelson and Cambie Sts., and Pacific Blvd. See Neighbourhoods.*

◆ **Broadway District** – *Broadway and 4th Ave., roughly from Oak St. west to Arbutus St.* Vancouver's most extensive retail area is a mile-long stretch of Broadway and 4th Avenue, south of False Creek. The district is chockablock with stores, cafes and galleries, virtually all of which are independent; many concentrate on locally made or Canadian goods. Some of the beautifully shaped confections at **Chocolate Arts** *(1620 W. 3rd Ave.; 604-739-0475 or 877-739-0475; www.chocolatearts.com)* bear First Nations designs—eagles, orcas, ravens—but they pose an existential dilemma: eating the chocolate destroys the art. Check out the seasonal line; in autumn, for example, you can purchase scrumptious pumpkin pralines.

◆ **Denman Street** – *West End. See Neighbourhoods.*

Chocolate Arts

First Nations Art

Masks, carvings, wood panels and bentwood boxes made by Western Canada's First Nations artisans are among the world's most distinctive artworks, instantly recognizable and immensely valuable. Any collector would treasure a cedar panel with vividly etched and brightly coloured illustrations of the whales, bears, eagles and ravens that are significant spirits to British Columbia's coastal peoples. Especially hard to find (and hard to make) are bentwood boxes, in which the cedar panels are formed into four sides, usually adorned with discreet decorative designs. Native art is the subject of some controversy, though: not all is made by First Nations people (non-authentic stores have been known to show "made in China" labels); and not all is even very good. If you care about the authenticity of a piece, your best course is to buy at a top-quality, reputable dealer—and expect to pay top dollar. Of course, what you get is the equal, in aesthetic and financial value, of any fine European or American painting. The best Inuit soapstone sculptures and Northwest Coast masks and wall panels can cost many thousands of dollars.

Best Outlets for First Nations Art

• **Marion Scott Gallery** *(2423 Granville St., Gastown; 604-685-1934; www.marionscottgallery.com)* has an especially fine selection of Inuit stone and ivory carvings, as well as prints.

• **Spirit Wrestler Gallery** *(47 Water St.; Gastown; 604-669-8813 or 888-669-8813; www.spiritwrestler.com)* specializes in Inuit carving and

Must Not Take Home

One of the great attractions of Vancouver shopping—for some Americans, at least—is that Cuban rum and cigars are freely available. US customs officials at Vancouver airports and the border are ever on the watch for these items. But it's perfectly legal to puff away on an Uppmann cigar or imbibe Havana Club rum while in Canada. Just make sure you dispose of contents, bottles and wrappers before you leave the country.

Northwest Coast masks, and also carries New Zealand Maori pieces.

• **Hill's Native Art** *(165 Water St., Gastown; 604-685-4249 or 866-685-5422; www.hillsnativeart.com)* is the most reputable dealer for less expensive First Nations art, and stocks boxes, masks, totems and other carvings. There are branch stores in Victoria, Nanaimo and Duncan.

• **Eagle Spirit Gallery** *(1803 Maritime Mews, Granville Island; 604-801-5277 or 888-801-5277; www.eaglespiritgallery.com)* features superlative Northwest Coast masks and totems, all splendidly displayed.

Richmond

• **International Travel Maps** *(12300 Bridgeport Rd. 604-273-1400)* does a mostly online business, but the company has a large warehouse-style store in Richmond. A huge selection of travel books and maps makes it a popular place place to shop.

NIGHTLIFE

Though Vancouver is a film- and music-industry capital, raves and disco just don't cut it here. Search out Vancouver's nightlife in the low-key lounges of the city's major hotels, and in myriad small restaurant/ nightclubs, where you can see live performers. For the complete scoop on Vancouver nightlife, pick up a free copy of the alternative weekly newspaper, *Georgia Straight*, or check the Thursday entertainment section of the *Vancouver Sun*.

Bacchus Lounge

845 Hornby St., in the Wedgewood Hotel, Downtown. 604-608-5319. www.wedgewoodhotel.com/ hotel/bacchus.

When you see the languorous painting of Bacchus that hangs over the piano in this elegant restaurant and nightspot, you'll know its prevailing philosophy: indulge yourself, peacefully. Jazz musicians ply the keyboards here most nights of the week. The relaxed setting encourages conversation; and the adjacent, fully enclosed cigar lounge draws athletes and celebrities alike. Needless to say, upscale Bacchus is a popular watering hole with the after-work crowd as well.

Gerard Lounge

845 Burrard St., in the Sutton Place Hotel, Downtown. 604-682-5511. www.vancouver.suttonplace.com.

This nightspot's clubby, quiet ambience within the luxurious Sutton Place Hotel is legendary for attracting film celebrities—and you can indeed spot stars here. Its low-key atmosphere also makes the lounge a comfortable space to sit and talk.

Irish Heather

210 Carrall St., Gastown. 604-688-9779. www.irishheather.com.

This gastropub/club is a great place to hear one of Vancouver's most popular genres—Celtic

The Irish Heather

Courtesy of The Irish Heather

900 West Lounge

©Fairmont Hotels & Resorts

music. Irish Heather features live performers most nights, including occasional appearances by well-known local bands.

900 West Lounge

900 W. Georgia St., in the Hotel Vancouver, Downtown. 604-669-9378. www.fairmont.com/ hotelvancouver.

Downtown's largest adult lounge encompasses a vast open space in the glitzy Art Moderne lobby of the venerable Hotel Vancouver. Jazz pianists and vocal artists entertain nightly, and hors-d'oeuvres and tapas are available from the hotel restaurant.

Railway Club

579 Dunsmuir St., Downtown. 604-681-1625. www.therailway club.com.

Lines are often long to get into this live-rock and alternative-music emporium that's been in business since 1931. And if you aren't dressed right (don't show up in your rodeo duds or three-piece suit), you might as well go someplace else.

River Rock Casino Resort

8811 River Rd., Richmond. 604-247-8900. www.riverrock.com.

The spiffy new building that houses this complex of entertainment and business venues creates an image of tradition and excitement. Inside you'll find the typical casino accoutrements, but beyond that, it's a fairly priced hotel with top-notch dining facilities, an Absolute Spa, and a convention and meeting centre. World-class stand-up comics perform on the main stage, interspersed with well-known musical acts from yesteryear and today. It's a comprehensive location for fun and business rolled into one.

Richard's on Richards

1036 Richards St., Downtown. 604-687-6794. www.richardson richards.com.

Vancouver's most conspicuous dance club offers DJ music every

Railway Club

©Steve Silman

night, with a rotating schedule of styles from hip-hop to electronica. Live bands perform on weekends and for special appearances. The club also books periodic hip-hop comedy nights.

Yale Hotel

1300 Granville St., Yaletown. 604-681-9253. www.theyale.ca.

Blues, issuing forth from both Canadian and American bands, is the theme here. The stage in this Victorian-era building has hosted international stars such as Bonnie Raitt, Buddy Guy and Elvin Bishop. Undergoing extensive renovations during early 2013, this venue promises to be a major draw in its newest phase of entertainment.

Yaletown Brewing Co.

1111 Mainland St., Yaletown. 604-681-2739. www.drinkfresh beer.com.

Yaletown's leading sports bar is a boisterous place to be on hockey night, and before and after games at BC Place Stadium and Rogers Arena. Pub-style food here is supplemented by house-made ales, stouts and other hearty brews. It's a great place to go if you want to be part of the crowd, and a lively one at that.

When the Stars Come Out

With an average of a half-dozen film productions underway at any given time in Vancouver, star-gazing is a popular pastime. The best places in the city for seeing stars are: the **Bacchus Lounge**, in the Wedgewood Hotel *(see above)*; **Gotham Steakhouse** downtown *(615 Seymour St.; 604-605-8282; www.gothamsteakhouse.com)*; **Joe Fortes Seafood & Chop House** in the West End *(777 Thurlow St.; 604-669-1940; www.joefortes.ca; see Restaurants)*; and Yaletown's **Elbow Room Cafe** *(560 Davie St.; 604-685-3628; www.theelbowroomcafe.com)* for a late breakfast.

Tonic Club

919 Granville St. 604-669-0469. www.thetonicclub.com.

Often rated at the top of Vancouver's litany of nightclubs, Tonic Club delivers three storeys of dancing, with the upper two serving as balconies that overlook the main dance floor. The 17-foot bar conjures up every cocktail imaginable while you dance to Latin and hip-hop tunes. Formerly The Paradise Theatre, Tonic Club has a VIP room that draws the city's elite to its upscale atmosphere.

Republic

958 Granville St. 604-669-3266. wwwdonnellygroup.ca

Committed to music and dance, this club rocks with live music and DJs 7 nights a week, opening at 9pm and hopping until the wee hours. Fashioned after the London genre of trendy clubs, it boasts two floors of thumping rhythm, the upper one offering table service for more discriminating clientele.

Bar None

1222 Hamilton St., Yaletown. 604-678-7000. www.donnelly group.ca/locations/night-clubs/ bar-none

With almost a homey feel, thanks to its natural brick walls, wood accents and cosy leather banquettes, Bar None attracts countless celebrities to its New York-style ambience. Live bands play here, but most of the Top 40, dance, house and hip-hop is spun by resident or guest DJs. Do yourself a favour and call ahead to be placed on the guest list.

GAY NIGHTLIFE

Celebrities Night Club

1022 Davie St., Downtown. 604-681-6180. www.celebrities nightclub.com.

Recently renovated, with state-of-the art sound, this club offers a weekly lineup and two floors for dancing and bars.

The Oasis Pub

1240 Thurlow St., West End. 604-685-1724. www.theoasispub.com.

Customers here enjoy a huge selection of tapas and martinis, accompanied by piano music; check out "Queer Improv" nights for wicked comedy and laughs.

Fountainhead Pub

1025 Davie St. 604-687-2222. www.thefountainheadpub.com.

Although it's famed for drawing a discriminating clientele, the Fountainhead is nonetheless somewhat unpretentious and surprisingly affordable. It's a pub, after all, open for lunch, with a variety of beer on tap. The covered patio is especially delightful in the warm weather.

Shine Night Club

364 Water St., Gastown. 604-408-4321 www.shinenightclub.com.

Known for turning its "spinners" into international stars of the DJ scene, this venue is one of the city's more vibrant clubs. The music is mostly hip-hop, but if you'd rather chill than dance, one of its two rooms is set aside as a more laid-back lounge.

NIGHTLIFE

SPAS

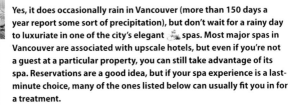

Yes, it does occasionally rain in Vancouver (more than 150 days a year report some sort of precipitation), but don't wait for a rainy day to luxuriate in one of the city's elegant 🛁 spas. Most major spas in Vancouver are associated with upscale hotels, but even if you're not a guest at a particular property, you can still take advantage of its spa. Reservations are a good idea, but if your spa experience is a last-minute choice, many of the ones listed below can usually fit you in for a treatment.

DAY SPAS

Absolute Spa at the Century

1015 Burrard St., at the Century Plaza Hotel. 604-684-2772. www.absolutespa.com.

Located in the lower level of the Century Plaza Hotel in mid-downtown, the Absolute pioneered the spa industry in Vancouver. Its fine reputation and established clientele combine to make it hard to get into at the last minute. If you do get in, you'll find a full menu of pampering here, from facials and manicures to mud wraps—in addition to such complementary services as light meals, eucalyptus steam, and an ozone-treated pool. Got jet lag? Absolute has three branch operations at Vancouver International Airport (two in the terminals and one at the Fairmont Vancouver Airport Hotel). Two more locations of Absolute have opened recently, one at the River Rock Casino Resort complex in Richmond, and another at Park Royal Mall in North Vancouver. There is also an Absolute Spa at the Fairmont Hotel Vancouver *(see below)*.

Vida Spa, The Sutton Place Hotel Vancouver

845 Burrard St., at the Sutton Place Hotel. 604-642-2999. www.vancouver.suttonplace.com.

Yes, those Hollywood types do like to pamper themselves. Vida Spa's host hotel is Sutton Place, a huge favourite with the film industry. Vida has long experience in taking care of discriminating spa clientele who demand the most gratifying, most comprehensive and most effective body treatments. Accordingly, the spa's stone

Ancient Cedars Spa

At the Wickaninnish Inn, Tofino (see Hotels). Located on the lower level of the oceanside lodge near Pacific Rim National Park Reserve, the spa at the **Wickaninnish Inn** sports a saltwater theme, utilizing thalassotherapy, seaweed wraps, sea-salt scrubs and the like to reflect the environment just out the door. The surroundings are exquisite—a leisurely hour-long walk on the long, sandy beach is the perfect way to conclude an afternoon of spa pampering.

MUST DO

The Spa at the Wedgewood Hotel

massage utilizes 54 hot stones and 18 cool ones to both relax and re-energize tired muscles. Treat yourself to the ultimate package, which combines a massage, facial, manicure, pedicure, reflexology and—ah, Hollywood—winds up with a champagne lunch.

Absolute Spa at The Fairmont Hotel Vancouver

900 W. Georgia St. 604-648-2909. www.fairmont.com.

The Fairmont's spa treatments include wraps, facials and infusions using Canadian rose-hip oil, whose healing properties are substantial. Try one of the European kur treatments, which replenish your body's lost nutrients using thermal mineral water, sea salts from France, mineral-rich moor mud and purifying algae.
If you want to work up a sweat before your massage, the facility includes fitness equipment along with saunas, a whirlpool, and swimming pools.

The Spa at the Wedgewood Hotel

845 Hornby St., at the Wedgewood Hotel. 604-608-5340. www.wedgewoodhotel.com.

Vancouver's best-known boutique hotel boasts a spa that draws on the hotel's international flavour for its character. The all-natural Epicuren line of skin products, used in facials, scrubs and other treatments, is designed to stimulate the body's immune system. Other distinctive treatments include Lavender Body Bliss, a scrub, wrap and lotion application all using lavender essence. Try the eucalyptus steam treatment after your workout in the fitness centre. The Spa at the Wedgewood won the prestigious 2012 Consumers Choice award for best day spa in the Vancouver area. Indulge!

SPAS

Skoah

1007 Hamilton St. 604-642-0200 or 888-697-5624. www.skoah.com.

The focus in this hip Yaletown spa is on skin care for the head and back. Try "sunny side down," a facial for your back with cleansing, exfoliation, detoxification and massage. The "up and down" combines facials for both head and back. Treatments here are more reasonably priced than at the big hotel spas. New locations include North Vancouver, Kitsilano, 2737 Granville St., and Metrotown.

Vida Spa

In Sheraton Vancouver Wall Centre Hotel, 1088 Burrard St. 604-682-8410; 800-401-4018 (Canada) or 888-865-2630 (USA). www.vidaspas.com.

Located in downtown Vancouver's largest hotel, Vida specializes in applying Ayurveda, the ancient Indian herbal wellness regime, to modern practices and techniques.

Body scrubs, wraps and massages utilizing Ayurvedic essences and lotions all induce a heightened sense of health and balance. Vida Spas are also located in Vancouver's Westin Bayshore Inn and at the Fairmont Château Whistler.

DESTINATION SPAS

These spa getaways blend Canada's Western ranching tradition with wholly modern health and wellness philosophies. BC's cattle-ranching district, the Cariboo, lies four to five hours away by car from Vancouver. The treatments you will experience at these ranches are worth the drive.

Echo Valley Ranch

On Jesmond Rd., in Clinton. 404km/251mi north of Vancouver. 250-459-2386 or 800-253-8831. www.evranch.com. 20 rooms.

A New Age retreat overlooking Fraser Canyon, this ranch ranks as a North American centre

Skoah, Yaletown

©skoah

Spa suite, Echo Valley Ranch

for the teaching and practice of Thai massage. Here you'll don lightweight pajamas for a "work out" of stretches and limb extensions with the assistance of a skillful therapist. A hydro treatment might follow. A day of horseback riding, a pampering massage and the lodge's Austrian-inspired cuisine all induce a sense of serenity as you watch the sun set over the Chilcotin Mountains.

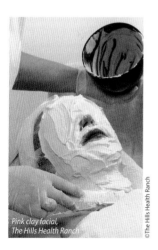

Pink clay facial, The Hills Health Ranch

The Hills Health Ranch

On Hwy. 97 in the town of 108-Mile Ranch. 487km/302mi north of Vancouver. 250-791-5225 or 800-668-2233. www.spabc.com. 46 units.

This health retreat/guest ranch draws clients from all over North America, and often on a repeat basis. They come for intensive rejuvenation and weight-loss programs here that combine exercise, recreation in the Cariboo parkland, body treatments and healthy cuisine. The ranch's signature rose-hip oil, made from rose hips actually gathered each fall in the area, is a superlative therapeutic lotion. All meals from the kitchen are prepared with nutritious ingredients designed to promote your fitness and general well being. Recreational activities include horseback riding, **hiking and biking** on surrounding trails threading the 20,000 acres of ranch property.

SPAS

RESTAURANTS

The venues listed below were selected for their ambience, location and/or value for money. Rates indicate the average cost of an appetizer, an entrée and a dessert for one person (not including tax, gratuity or beverages). Most restaurants are open daily and accept major credit cards. Call for information regarding reservations, dress code and opening hours. Restaurants listed are located in Vancouver unless otherwise noted. For a complete listing of restaurants mentioned in this guide, see the Index.

| *Luxury* | **$$$$** over $75 | *Moderate* | **$$** $25 to $50 |
| *Expensive* | **$$$** $50 to $75 | *inexpensive* | **$** less than $25 |

VANCOUVER

Luxury

Le Crocodile

©Le Crocodile

Le Crocodile
$$$$ **French**
909 Burrard St. 604-669-4298.
www.lecrocodilerestaurant.com.
If you don't mind eating beneath the gaze of a smiling crocodile, this place will delight you. Though the room has an urban shopping-plaza sensibility (down to the parquet flooring), its white tablecloths, table lamps, and red and russet accents give the space charm. When it's full, which it mostly is, ambience is created by the "ahhs" of the patrons. For more than 25 years, Le Crocodile has offered a

fusion of classic French cuisine with West Coast nuances. The five-course chef's tasting menu is uber-popular, especially when paired with wines. Dont' miss dessert: try the crêpes with hazelnut mousse.

Yew Restaurant
$$$$ **Contemporary**
791 W. Georgia St., in the Four Seasons Hotel. 604-692-4939.
www.yewrestaurant.com.
Definitely an upscale restaurant with options for lower-priced dining, Yew lets you go wild in your selections, or moderate and still enjoy a superb meal. It defines its menus, which include vegan dinner and lunch dishes, as modern coastal. Serving breakfast, lunch and dinner at tree-top level, Yew has a communal dining table (great if you're eating alone); the decor is dressed in a slick combination of warm wood and glass. The wine cellar, central to the room, is made of glass and metal. Sundays deliver half-off bottled wine, a real deal, especially given that this is a high-end hotel. Try the luscious paella as an appetizer, followed by one of several perfectly prepared fish dishes, and topped off with either a s'mores dessert, or unique mini-éclairs with a purposely kitschy look.

Bacchus

$$$ **French**
845 Hornby St., in the
Wedgewood Hotel. 604-608-5319.
www.wedgewoodhotel.com.

The contemporary French dishes here rely heavily on West Coast ingredients. Roast rosemary-studded lamb, top-grade steak, and regional fish such as BC salmon, Haida Gwaii halibut filets, sablefish and Alaskan scallops typify the changing menu. The dessert standout, crème brûlée is presented in clever combinations like cardamom and ginger with poached pear. Luxurious upholstery, dark woods and Venetian-glass lamps above the tables help create the muted, refined atmosphere. Brunch and afternoon tea are served on weekends, and the lounge features live entertainment in the evenings.

Bishop's

$$$ **West Coast**
2183 W. 4th Ave. 604-738-2025.
www.bishopsonline.com.
Dinner only.

John Bishop is widely credited with inaugurating modern fine dining in Vancouver when he opened his namesake restaurant in Kitsilano, after studying under master chef and local notable, Umberto Menghi. Bishop himself still greets diners most nights, and personable service distinguishes the low-key, white-tablecloth setting. The menu is a changing array of West Coast innovation, typified by cross-cultural entrées like local roast duck breast, rack of lamb, scallops and beef tenderloin, and for dessert, vanilla bean risotto as a change of pace.

Blue Water Cafe + Raw Bar

$$$ **Seafood**
1095 Hamilton St.
Dinner only. 604-688-8078.
www.bluewatercafe.net.

Blue Water artfully presents wild-sourced and sustainable gourmet seafood that is exceptional. The signature dish, the appetizer tower, rises as a multilevel set of trays with about a dozen treats piled on it—shrimp, ahi tuna, oysters, crabcakes, roe, sushi rolls and clams, to name a few. Many diners order only this dish for dinner. The raw bar offers fine sushi in this "east meets west" establishment. Main dishes are expertly cooked fish filets, ranging from salmon to shark. But save room for the lemon tart. Warm wood tones and side lighting create an elegant atmosphere in this reconfigured Yaletown warehouse, where the bar is open late.

C Restaurant

$$$ **Seafood**
1600 Howe St. 604-681-1164.
www.crestaurant.com.

C chef and co-owner Robert Clark stood the seafood world on its head when he conjured

Bishop's

©Jordi Sancho

up such unorthodox delicacies as seared scallops wrapped in octopus bacon. Smoked black cod (sablefish), whole fish steamed in tea, caviar wrapped in gold foil, and gorgonzola cheesecake number among other signature dishes. But it's not all exotic. There are options for those with more timid palates such as the lean flat iron steak (order it medium or less) and the classic fish and chips with minted peas and tarta sauce. Clark's commitment to serving local, sustainable seafood means that he bypasses the middleman and purchases directly from the fishermen. The minimalist black and white decor is airy (a visit to the whimsically decorated bathrooms is a must), and the patio overlooking False Creek is the best seat in the house on sunny days.

🦐 Cioppino's Mediterapean Grill

$$$ **Italian**

1133 Hamilton St. 604-688-7466. www.cioppinosyaletown.com.
Attentive service reaches its peak at this high-end Yaletown restaurant. The "Cucina Naturale" Italian-style cuisine, low in animal fats, is exceptional, with pastas, risottos and the namesake seafood stew weighting the dinner menu. For dessert, try the chef's version of classic tiramisu, resplendent with mascarpone, dark chocolate sorbet and a coffee macaroon. Book extra time to allow perusal of the 62-page wine list, a regular mention in *Wine Spectator*. But what's most memorable is the array of waiters—up to a half dozen per table—ready to spring into action. The open, exhibition kitchen

seems impossibly busy, with a small army of cooks and waiters hustling in and out. Somehow it all works. This renovated warehouse features huge beams overhead, but the industrial feel is softened by cherry-wood trim. Bill Clinton and Wayne Gretzky are among the fans of this award-winning establishment.

Diva

$$$ **West Coast**

645 Howe St., in the Metropolitan Hotel. 604-602-7788. www.metropolitan.com/diva.
One of the birthplaces of Vancouver's West Coast cuisine, this restaurant features an open kitchen, some 500 wines, a five-course tasting menu, and a chef's table for a singular dining experience. With warm wood and subdued accents, several levels of well-lit dining floors make Diva a place to see and be seen; it's especially popular for pre-theatre dinners and brunch. Signature dishes include smoked black cod, gently braised; fish is dominant on the menu. The after-dinner cheese course is one of the most extensive in North America, with a wide selection of European, American and Canadian artisanal cheeses.

Fleuri

$$$ **West Coast**

845 Burrard St., in the Sutton Place Hotel. 604-642-2900. www.vancouver.suttonplace.com.
The menu here is one of the city's finest and most comprehensive, offering something for almost all tastes. Chicken, fish, pork, lamb and beef are all presented with optimum artistry and creative accompaniments. The BC steelhead

(trout) is especially succulent and flavourful. This hotel dining room serves breakfast, lunch and dinner in its gracious, classical setting that makes a genteel backdrop for the artful cuisine.

Imperial Chinese Seafood Restaurant

$$$ **Chinese**
355 Burrard St. 604-688-8191. www.imperialrest.com.
One of the most elegant dining rooms in Vancouver, this restaurant features a grand entrance, tables overlooking Coal Harbour and a high, arched ceiling dotted with chandeliers. The Marine Building in which it is housed is a world-class Art Deco shrine. Cantonese fare matches the atmosphere—high-style Mandarin dishes such as Peking duck, sautéed lobster and crab, and sizzling beef and pineapple. Dim sum is available at lunch. The attentive staff is multi-lingual and well-versed in formal service.

Joe Fortes Seafood & Chop House

$$$ **Seafood**
777 Thurlow St. 604-669-1940. www.joefortes.ca.
Joe's specialty is raw oysters—more than a dozen kinds on most nights, affording diners the chance to savour the taste differences between oysters grown in a variety of waters. The clubby, dark-wood atmosphere lends a chophouse air to this West End haunt. Among the 50 varieties of fish served, the best entrées are simply grilled or pan-seared filets of halibut, cod, salmon and rockfish. Hand-cut steaks and chops round out the meaty menu. Combine turf with surf for a personalized meal. In business for nearly three decades, Joe's has achieved legend status, and the onion rings are the best in Vancouver (and may be part of the reason as well as the great wine list).

Lift

$$$ **Contemporary**
333 Menchions Mews. 604-689-5438. www.liftbarandgrill.com.
Housed in a sleek two-storey building that seems to float over Coal Harbour, this restaurant is a see-and-be-seen location. Lift turns out consistently delightful urban food and serves a wide variety of wines, many of those vinted in BC. Meat-lovers will go mad for the terrine appetizer with quail, venison, foie gras and rabbit. Or "whets" as the establishment calls them. The main courses span all forms of meat, poultry and fish, with a feature dish being the cornmeal-crusted Arctic char; and there's always sushi available. With its spacious outdoor deck, this sophisticated spot is open for lunch, brunch on weekends, and dinner every night.

Miku

$$$ **Japanese**
1055 W. Hastings St. 604-568-3900. www.mikurestaurant.com.
More than just another sushi joint, Miku serves *aburi* sushi and other top-end Japanese cuisine that runs the creative gamut from high-style raw dishes to Sumiyaki-grilled meats, served in a minimalist modern decor. Dishes are presented with maximum artistry and signature desserts, such as greet tea tiramisu, are literally works of art. The sweeping marble

bar creates a focal point in the sleek space. Open for lunch and dinner with a varied wine list to complement the singular dishes.

Moderate

Adesso Bistro
$$ **Italian**
1906 Haro St. (near Gilford). 604-568-9975. www.adessobistro.net No lunch Mon–Fri.
This West End eatery follows the local culinary tradition of Italy's region of Liguria, and tosses in a little contemporary spice for added flair. The word translates more or less as "momentarily," and indeed the food is served fresh as can be. Unpretentious and lively, the owners, by their own admission, have used "love, tradition and soul," not glitz and glamour, to create a homey, happy atmosphere with dependably delicious dishes. Among the house specialties is superb *aragosta*, mascarpone-and-whisky risotto with lobster. Patrons rave about the pasta, and often cite the garlicky *linguine alle vorgole* (clams) with white wine and herbs as a favourite. Open for dinner 7 days a week and brunch on the weekends.

Bitter
$$ **British**
16 W. Hastings St., Gastown (near Carrall). 604-558-4658. www.bittertastingroom.com.
While British cuisine may seem an oxymoron, the emphasis here is handcrafted BC beers, and a snack-style menu that balances well with the various levels of brew bitterness. The eight taps offer a revolving selection of beers; be sure to sample the Stumpy coffee porter, an exclusive to Bitters. Of course there are cocktails and wine available, but beer rules, and the menu that supports it includes a tasting platter that dishes up sausage, cheese and mackerel, a unique ploughman's lunch plate, and yummy cheese-stuffed Yorkshire puddings.

Cardero's
$$ **Seafood**
1583 Coal Harbour Quay. 604-669-7666. www.carderos.com.
Perched on a pier over Coal Harbour, between downtown and Stanley Park, Cardero's is famed for "fish, chops and a wok."
The up-tempo menu hews to seafood mainstays—you can't go wrong with the fish and chips, the grilled salmon is done just right, and the shrimp-topped Caesar salad does justice to both salads and seafood. Call ahead for a window table to get the best view for supping tapas, grilled meat, fresh fish, pizza and pasta, and on occasion, fresh Atlantic lobster. Almost every diner is treated to a luminescent view of the yachts moored at the nearby marina.

CinCin Ristorante
$$ **Italian**
1154 Robson St. 604-688-7338. www.cincin.net.
Mustard- and blood-orange-colored stucco walls, brick trim and wood-fired ovens combine to give this bustling bistro a warm, Mediterranean air, a cross between a grotto and a courtyard. The stylish Italian cuisine melds traditional dishes with gourmet embellishments—classic *ossobuco alla Milanese*, pastas and risottos, pizzas cooked in the wood-

fired oven, and shellfish pots. Ingredients are distinctly sourced in Canada, and the kitchen offers gluten-free pizza, bread and pasta.

Pink Pearl

$$ **Chinese**
1132 E. Hastings St. 604-253-4316.
www.pinkpearl.com.

Every morning at the crack of dawn, the dim sum cooks arrive at Pink Pearl to start preparing the day's delicacies. Every day near noon, cars and taxis start to pull up, disgorging workers from downtown who come for a dim sum lunch. By 12:30pm the vast room is packed, and the dim sum ladies are plying the aisles with baskets and plates of dumplings, rolls, cakes and stuffed pastries—vegetarian, seafood, fruit- or meat-filled; rice, wheat or taro flour; hot, sweet, sour or all three. By 2pm, the day's selection is depleted, so don't come late.

The Sandbar

$$ **Seafood**
1535 Johnson St., Granville Island. 604-669-9030. www.vancouver dine.com/sandbar.

Tucked under the Granville Street bridge, this cavernous 300-seat eatery is a hub of activity busy with waiters and a large kitchen staff; the mood is upbeat and lively. The specialty is fresh fish; lobster, crab and mussels are drawn directly from a tank of live shellfish and cooked a-la-minute. For diners who can't decide, prawns, lobster or crab can be added to a top-quality steak that's grilled to perfection. Try the cedar-planked West Coast salmon, a Sandbar specialty.

Sawasdee

$$ **Thai**
4250 Main St. 604-876-4030.
www.sawasdeethairestaurant.com.

Vancouver's first authentic Thai restaurant still excels at blending BC ingredients with Thai dishes. Duck curry is a standout; so is the green curry (with chicken or shrimp). Many diners consider Swasdee's pad Thai the city's best. The softly lit stucco interior lends a tropical air, and the menu offers that most wonderful of Thai desserts, black-rice pudding. Patrons are given the option to order their meals from mild to very hot, and are invariably thrilled with the presentations, often graced with flowers (mostly edible).

Shabusen Yakiniku House

$$ **Japanese/Korean**
755 Burrard St. (at 14th Ave). 604-669-3883. www.shabusen.com.

This eatery is hopping at lunchtime, so arrive early or make reservations. You can order from the menu, but most in the know choose the buffet, and use the BBQ grill in the middle of the tables to cook their own selection. For lighter fare—or as appetizers for a full meal—the sushi selection is among the best in town. Shabusen specializes in Japanese "Yakiniku" cuisine.

Vij's

$$ **Indian**
1480 W. 11th Ave. 604-736-6664.
www.vijs.ca. Dinner only.

Diners literally make pilgrimages here from across Canada to experience Vikram Vij's edgy Indian cuisine. The no-reservations policy means dinner hopefuls line up early, by 5pm for the

5:30pm opening, and wait patiently to experience the lovely, aromatic atmosphere. What's the draw? The astounding culinary inventions, such as buttermilk curry, ghee-braised short ribs in a red-wine-cinnamon curry, or lamb "popsicles" in cream curry. The seafood selection is traditional Indian, limited largely to prawns, but there are lots of vegetarian options on the seasonal menu.

Inexpensive

La Bretagne Crêperie
$ **French**
795 Jervis St. (at Robson) 604-688-5989.
Crêpes are simple in concept—egg-and-flour batter, lightly sautéed, folded and filled. It's the execution that demands skill. This West End cafe's new owner hails from France and speaks primarily French. Crêpes here are traditional (you can get buckwheat flour) and very, very light. If you want dinner, have your crêpes filled with ham and cheese; for dessert, choose apples or Nutella; or at breakfast, ask for ham and well, cheese again. Crêpes make a quick, tasty meal, but if a crêpe is not filling enough, start with the signature French onion soup. French hard ciders and wines round out the menu.

Stepho's Souvlaki Greek Taverna
$ **Greek**
1124 Davie St. 604-683-2555.
Sometimes the line to get into Stepho's stretches out the door, down the street and around the corner at lunch and dinner. All those people come for heaping platters of Greek roast lamb,

potatoes, salad and vegetables—an utterly filling, yet economical meal that will last all day. Yes, they have baklava, but it's hard to find the room for it after finishing off a dinner platter.

Vera's Burger Shack
$ **American**
1181 Denman St. 604-681-5450; www.verasburgershack.com (multiple locations including Kitsilano, Granville, Gastown and North Vancouver).
Vancouver burger-lovers know they can count on one of the several Vera's locations for their fix—and hungry kids craving something quick and "normal" will leave satisfied without breaking the bank. Now franchising outside of British Columbia, the chain offers hot dogs, sandwiches, fries and soft drinks too.

VANCOUVER ISLAND

Luxury

🏕 Sooke Harbour House
$$$$ **West Coast**
Whiffen Spit Rd., Sooke: Hwy. 14 west from Victoria. 250-642-3421 or 800-889-9688. www.sooke harbourhouse.com. 28 rooms.
When Sinclair and Frederique Philip opened a small inn in the mid-1970s to offer New Wave cuisine based on exotic, local ingredients, virtually no one in Canada was exploring those culinary frontiers. Today an entire cuisine (West Coast) borrows their pioneering principles, and Sooke Harbour House has become quite simply one of the the most famous restaurants in Canada. Gourmands fly across the continent to have

dinner here. What they find every night is different, but always draws on local seafood (like oysters, sea cucumbers, rockfish, seaweed), artisanal cheeses, and fresh vegetables (like foraged mushrooms), herbs and fruits grown in the inn's extensive gardens. Supplies of such foods are limited, and the menu can change during the course of an evening.

Expensive

Bengal Lounge
$$$ **Indian**
721 Government St., in the Empress Hotel, Victoria. 250-389-2727. www.fairmont.com/empress-victoria/dining/thebengallounge.
The Empress Hotel's less-formal dining room is redolent with Empire atmosphere—polished mahogany, ceiling fans, potted palms, red-leather armchairs, even a tiger skin on the wall. The lounge dates back to the 1950s, and is noted for its inventive array of martinis and tropical drinks and its splendid selection of curries. At lunch and dinner, a long table is laden with ingredients for the curry buffet, ranging from coconut-chicken to mango chutney. At both meals, à la carte offerings include curry flambé. The Bengal Lounge features live jazz Friday and Saturday evenings, but don't turn up in ripped jeans, cut-offs or baseball caps; this dignified place definitely has a dress code.

Café Brio
$$$ **Italian**
944 Fort St., Victoria. 250-383-0009. www.café-brio.com. Dinner only.
A decade after pioneering bistro cuisine in Victoria, Café Brio finds its popularity unabated. The intriguing decor (Modigliani-style nudes on the walls, unadorned fir-plank floors, 18-feet ceilings) serves as a backdrop for excellent Northern Italian cooking. Braised breast of veal, and scallops on rosemary polenta are typical dishes, but the menu changes often, and the signature pasta dishes are not to be missed. Groups or families will enjoy the Sharing Menu that offers six dishes, selected by the chef, and is served family-style. Some of the more sought after booths are reserved weeks ahead in peak season.

Paprika Bistro
$$$ **French**
2524 Estevan Ave., Victoria. 250-592-7424. www.paprika-bistro.com. Dinner only.
Neighbourhood bistros have risen like Victoria's spring flowers in the capital city over the past decade; Paprika is the best of the bunch, situated just 10 minutes from downtown on Oak Bay. The French provincial cuisine relies on fresh island ingredients—farm-grown duck, lamb and pork; fresh-picked wild mushrooms; seafood from the Strait of Georgia. A sumptuous bisque, either shellfish or lobster, starts the meal every evening. Simply roasted or braised meats and fish mark the entrée selections. Sample the good selection of BC wines, and be sure to check out the daily handmade pasta feature.

Moderate

Ming's
$$ **Chinese**
1321 Quadra St., Victoria. 250-385-4405. www.mings.ca. Dinner only.
Though it occasionally ventures into Szechuan or Hunan cuisine, Ming's serves classic Mandarin dishes in Victoria's Chinatown. After entering the dining room through an ivory moongate, you'll find that the service is infinitely attentive, and all the usuals are on the menu, from sweet-and-sour pork to fried rice. The most interesting dishes include sweet-and-sour duck, ginger beef, and a scrumptious Buddhist delicacy, vegetarian *lo han jai*. The restaurant offers delivery service if you'd rather eat in your hotel.

Spinnaker's Gastro Brewpub
$$ **Pub Food**
308 Catherine St., Victoria. 250-386-2739. www.spinnakers.com.
Spinnaker's claims to be the first licenced brewpub in Canada—a distinction it enhances considerably with this restaurant perched beside the Inner Harbour. The heritage Craftsman building includes the brewpub, restaurant, outdoor deck, tap room and a sundries shop in which you can buy such marvels as malt vinegar made from Spinnaker's ale. Dining fare is upscale pub food, such as a tasting plate of island artisan cheeses, a braised-lamb sandwich, and yeast-battered fish and chips. The brews are highly flavoured, and very, very fresh. Try the housemade thin-crust pizza direct from the wood oven, and order the elderflower cheesecake for dessert.

Inexpensive

Blue Fox Cafe
$ **American**
919 Fort St., Victoria. 250-380-1683. Breakfast and Lunch only.
It's easy to find the Blue Fox: just look for the line out on the sidewalk, especially for weekend breakfasts or weekday lunches. The fare here is not exotic—breakfast platters piled high with hotcakes, thick toast, fat omelettes and sausages. Lunch means big handmade hamburgers and hand-cut fries and meatloaf. Breakfast is served all day, if your patience is tested by the morning lines. Because Blue Fox is so busy, don't expect to be in and out in half an hour; the service pace tends to align with how packed the place is. Be prepared to wait.

Common Loaf Bake Shop
$ **American**
180 First St., Tofino. 250-725-3915.
The loaves at this counterculture hangout in Tofino (but visitors of all persuasions are drawn to the popular spot) are far from common—the thick and nutty multi-grain concoctions are a meal in themselves. There's also excellent coffee, and a lineup of luscious pastries, muffins and scones in the morning from the bakery side of the cafe. At lunch and dinner *(the latter served only til 6pm in winter)*, simple soups and salads are offered on the menu. The cedar-and-fir panelled interior is pure New Age, and the bulletin board is the place to find out what's happening in the West Coast alternative community, from Reiki classes to logging protests.

MUST EAT

Fine Dining in the Wilds of BC

Artisanal food and wine tours "in the most unlikely places" are offered by the unique tour company, Swallowtail Tours. From a one-day Vancouver-area wine tour for $39 to a 3-day boutique winery tour, the budding sommelier traveller will find singular wines produced in small batches before they get snapped up by eager restaurateurs and chefs. These winery tours go in-depth, helping wine lovers make the connection between what they sip and the terroir that delivers the grapes. Among the more popular and unusual tours of BC gourmet food and wine are the crab-cooking tour that features catching, cooking and eating dungeness crab right on the beach, and the foraging tour to secret spots where you'll find (and eat!) salmonberries, wild mushrooms and Indian rhubarb. For the ultimate in BC wine and food, a special tour has party members snowshoe to a mountain top that overlooks Vancouver for a 3-course meal served in the snow. All tours are guided. www.swallowtail.ca.

WHISTLER

Luxury

Rim Rock Cafe

$$$$ Contemporary
2117 Whistler Rd., Creekside (just outside the village of Whistler) 877-932-5589. www.rimrock whistler.com. Dinner only.

"Cafe" is something of a misnomer here at Whistler's favourite fine-dining establishment. Loved by locals as the special spot for birthdays and other celebrations, the Rim Rock has an extensive menu featuring fish and game. Popular since it opened in 1987, the restaurant more than makes up for limited culinary imagination with its consistency, atmosphere, and casual but excellent service. With two fireplaces, a patio and suitably rustic decor, Rim Rock exudes a warm sensibility and oozes comfort. Savour the lobster mashed potatoes or the mixed grill, both eternally popular. Dessert? Decadent, gooey sticky toffee pudding, of course.

Elements Urban Tapas Lounge

$$ Tapas
4359 Main St. (in the Summit Lodge). 604-932-5569. www.elementswhistler.com.

Just when you thought "BC" meant "bring cash," a restaurant comes along that encourages you to sup on as little or as much as you find comfortable. Open for breakfast, lunch and dinner, Elements delivers the best of eggs Benedict for the morning, and a substantial range of tapas options for an eclectic dinner collection, matched with boutique wines. The casual, warm decor suggests intimacy and laid-back dining, a suitable backdrop to the ever-changing, seasonal and locally sourced tapas menu. If you like beef, you'll love the perfectly prepared bison petit tender three ways. If you're vegetarian, there's plenty to choose from, too. The restaurant is owned by the people who own Whistler's well-regarded **Pacific Bistro** *(www.wildwoodrestaurants.ca)*, which is popular with locals and tourists alike.

HOTELS

The properties listed below were selected for their ambience, location and/or value for money. Prices (in Canadian Dollars) reflect the average cost for a standard double room for two people (not including applicable city or provincial taxes). Hotels in Vancouver constantly offer special discount packages, so it's best to check online. Price ranges quoted do not reflect the city hotel tax of 10 percent. Properties are located in Vancouver, unless otherwise specified.

Luxury	$$$$$	over $350
Expensive	$$$$	$250 to $350
Moderate	$$$	$175 to $250
Inexpensive	$$	$100 to $175
Budget	$	less than $100

VANCOUVER

Luxury

Fairmont Waterfront
$$$$$ 489 rooms
900 Canada Place. 604-691-1991 or 866-540-4509. www.fairmont. com/waterfront-vancouver.
The Waterfront is the Fairmont chain's downtown business hotel, a gleaming steel-and-glass tower in which every room has an expansive view—60 percent of the rooms overlook Burrard Inlet, Stanley Park and the North Shore. The rooms are furnished in crisp cream tones with gray and brown accents, maple and oak and marble. The hotel offers guided morning runs, a walkable roof-top herb garden, and for Fairmont Gold members, free valet parking, a private concierge, and inclusive breakfast and canapés in the evening. An extensive health club, business centre, shopping arcade and **Herons West Coast Kitchen + Bar ($$$)** round out the facilities. Canada Place sits across the street.

Four Seasons
$$$$$ 373 rooms
791 W. Georgia St. 604-689-9333 or 866-223-9333. www.fourseasons. com/vancouver.
Attentive service is the hallmark at this property, one of Vancouver's consistently top-rated hotels—if a doorman sees you returning

Lobby, Fairmont Waterfront

©Fairmont Hotels & Resorts

from a jog, he'll hand you a towel and water bottle. Though not overly large, the guest rooms are elegantly furnished, with brass trim, natural tones and marble baths. Hotel facilities are lavish, including an indoor-outdoor pool that opens out onto a huge second-storey garden terrace. The hotel boasts 24-hour multi-lingual concierge services and business centre, and claims to offer 300 wines by the glass!

Opus Hotel
$$$$$ **97 rooms**
322 Davie St. 604-642-6787 or 866-642-6787. www.opushotel.com.
Designers of this utterly distinctive hotel in Yaletown chose unusual decorative elements to echo the property's hip neighbourhood. Candles and settees are the lobby furnishings; headset-adorned staffers greet guests at reception podiums. Rooms feature strong colours such as purple and ebony, and bathrooms have floor-to-ceiling windows, and a counter made from a long stone slab. Rated among the top five trendy hotels in the world, this hotel is aimed directly at hipsters.

Fairmont Hotel Vancouver
$$$$ **557 rooms**
900 W. Georgia St. 604-684-3131 or 800-441-1414. www.fairmont.com.
The Hotel Van is a Canadian icon, one of the string of château-style landmark hotels spread across the country and built near its railroads about 100 years ago. Steep gables and copper roofs characterize the familiar Vancouver landmark. Rooms often contain unaltered historic elements such as tiled baths with deep soaking tubs. Every service imaginable is on-site, including a lavish health club with a glass-roofed pool and an Absolute Spa *(see SPAS)*. **Griffins (\$\$)** is undisputedly the best place for breakfast in downtown and offers a "decadent" buffet for other meals. Try 900 West Lounge for evening cocktails or afternoon tea. The hotel is pet-friendly and even has canine concierges.

Sutton Place Hotel
$$$$ **379 rooms**
845 Burrard St. 604-682-5511 or 866-378-8866. www.vancouver.suttonplace.com.
There's hardly a minute that no limousine is waiting in the

Executive suite, Opus Hotel
©Opus Hotel

driveway of the pink-toned palace on Burrard that remains the film industry's favourite place to stay in Vancouver. Snazzy guest rooms have huge picture windows, ivory and beige decor and marble baths in a classic luxury style. The service is expert and unquestioning, and every amenity imaginable is offered, from an extensive fitness facility to (naturally) 24-hour room service. The adjacent La Grande Residence is a 164-unit short-term luxury apartment complex.

Wedgewood Hotel

$$$$ 83 rooms
845 Hornby St. 604-689-7777 or 800-663-0666. www.wedgewood hotel.com.
Loyal fans of this discreet boutique hotel consider it one of Vancouver's best. Owner Eleni Skalbania chose the distinctive French and Italian decor for the spacious suites, outfitted with brocade-covered couches, in-room host bars and balconies overlooking the Law Courts. The

Wedgewood Hotel
©Wedgewood Hotel & Spa

service is attentive, and a spa complements the compact health club *(see Spas)*. Bacchus restaurant *(see Restaurants)* and lounge are on the ground floor. The Vancouver Art Gallery and Robson Street shopping are just minutes away. This property is a designated Relais & Châteaux hotel, but remains a family-run business.

Moderate

Granville Island Hotel

$$$ 85 rooms
1253 Johnston St. 604-683-7373 or 800-663-1840. www.granville islandhotel.com.
The white siding of this two-storey property evokes the sense of sails that float past Granville Island. The interior is utterly contemporary, with spacious rooms furnished in soothing neutrals. The hotel faces False Creek, and sits at the quiet end of its namesake island, where cafes, stalls and galleries are just minutes away. Amenities include a full health club, restaurant and bar, and three executive suites. Pets are welcome for a modest fee.
The Dockside Restaurant ($$) offers a Jazz and Blues brunch.

Hotel LeSoleil

$$$ 119 rooms
567 Hornby St. 604-632-3000 or 877-632-3030. www.lesolei lhotel.com.
The Old-World elegance of the lobby sets the tone at this lush downtown boutique hotel—voted in the top 25 luxury hotels in Canada by a much-used travel website. The cosy rooms continue this theme, with down-pillowed beds, Biedermeier-style furniture, brocade fabrics in gold and

crimson and hushed lighting. Its downtown location is close to Canada Place, Stanley Park, the Art Gallery and Gastown, and in the heart of the shopping, financial and business districts.

Listel Vancouver

$$$ **129 rooms**

1300 Robson St. 604-684-8461 or 800-663-5491. www.thelistel hotel.com.

Local art is the distinguishing element at this chic boutique hotel sitting on Robson Street. Rooms on gallery floors are decorated with works from the hotel's alliance with a nearby upscale art dealer; one floor features First Nations art derived from an affiliation with the UBC Museum of Anthropology *(see Museums)*. Spacious suites have Berber carpet, beige and maroon hues, and cosy window seats. The location is ideal for visiting Stanley Park and the Vancouver Art Gallery, and for watching the bustling scene on Robson. The hotel boasts a zero-waste policy, all smoke-free rooms and facilities, and complimentary wine receptions.

Pan Pacific

$$$ **503 rooms**

999 Canada Place. 604-662-8111 or 800-937-1515 (US), 800-663-1515 (Canada). www.vancouver. panpacific.com.

Perched on the shoreward end of the Canada Place pier, the Pan Pacific's white-sided tower faces water on three sides, so virtually all the rooms have expansive views of Burrard Inlet. Asian flair flavours the famously attentive service, which relies on a small army of staffers to meet guest needs. The neutrally decorated rooms are compact but luxuriously outfitted, with mahogany and marble touches. The hotel has direct accessibility to the Vancouver World Trade Centre, and prime shopping areas.

St. Regis

$$$ **72 rooms**

602 Dunsmuir St. 604-681-1135 or 800-770-7929. www.stregis hotel.com.

There's nothing fancy about the St. Regis, which opened in 1913, whose rooms are compact, furnished in muted gray tones, quiet and air-conditioned, but it's

Sortino suite, Listel Hotel

©Listel Hotel

HOTELS

Executive suite, St. Regis
©St. Regis Hotel

Venerable apple trees shade the backyard patio of this restored timber tycoon's North Shore mansion. The genteel 1920s Arts and Crafts-style house features stunning built-in cabinetry, especially in the formal dining room where guests enjoy sumptuous breakfasts of house-made pastries and preserves, omelettes or French toast. Guest rooms have eclectic furnishings such as walnut four-poster beds, and the honeymoon suite boasts a heated bathroom floor and a sitting room with fireplace.

Inexpensive

North Vancouver Hotel
$$ 71 rooms
1800 Capilano Rd., North Vancouver. 604-987-4461 or 800-663-4055. www.north vancouverhotel.ca.
This colourful stucco property is a top-notch motel with an excellent location. Spacious rooms, done in pastel fabrics, are situated in quiet buildings set back from the road. A palm-bordered swimming pool, free local calls, complimentary passes to a fitness club, on-site laundry facilities and a full hot breakfast round out the amenities. The setting is ideal for visiting Grouse Mountain, and lies within a half hour of the Horseshoe Bay ferry terminal. Pets are welcome in designated rooms for a surcharge.

Sylvia Hotel
$$ 120 rooms
1154 Gilford St. 604-681-9321 or 877-681-9321. www.sylviahotel.com.
Many is the family whose Sylvia loyalty spans generations. It is by far the best economical hotel

affordable, convenient and has its perks. The mid-downtown location is close to Canada Place, Gastown and Chinatown. The hotel offers these amenities free of charge: a business centre, Internet access (Wi-Fi), global long-distance phone calls, a full breakfast, and a sports club, but has no on-site parking.

Residences on Georgia
$$$ 493 rooms
1288 W. Georgia St. 604-891-6101. www.respal.com.
These sleek modern apartments are an ideal choice for longer-stay visitors to Vancouver. Furnished in muted gray, white, beige and brushed-metal trim, with small kitchenettes, breakfast nooks and small office spaces, they appeal to film-industry workers in town for shoots. Included are a screening room downstairs, access to a health club across the street, gated underground parking and private-access security. Weekly and monthly rates compare favourably to moderate hotel rates.

Thistledown House
$$$ 5 rooms
3910 Capilano Rd., North Vancouver. 604-986-7173 or 888-633-7173. www.thistle-down.com.

Sylvia Hotel

©Sylvia Hotel

in downtown Vancouver, and it's the one closest to Stanley Park to boot (with parking included). The rooms and suites are like mid-20C apartments, with polyglot furnishings, little discernible decor scheme, ample closets and sitting rooms. Many have kitchenettes—real ones, with refrigerators, stoves, sinks and counter space. The ivy-covered brick building is a World War I-era landmark, erected in 1912 as an apartment building, facing English Bay and the southeast end of the seawall pedestrian path. Pets are welcome.

Budget

Hostelling International
$ 282 rooms
*1025 Granville St. (Central);
604-685-5335 or 866-762-4122;
226 rooms. 1114 Burnaby St.
(Downtown); 604-684-4565 or
866-762-4122; 223 rooms. 1515
Discovery St. (Jericho Beach);
604-224-3208 or 866-762-4122.
www.hihostels.ca.*
All three of Vancouver's hostels offer excellent locations. Rooms (both dorm-style and private) are clean and updated. Full facilities

range from media rooms to laundries and cafes, as well as staff information services. The downtown location is on a quiet street near Stanley Park; the central location is handy to Granville Island, Gastown and the city's entertainment district. The Jericho Beach hostel is closest to Kitsilano and the University of British Columbia.

Shaughnessy Village
$ 240 rooms
*1125 W. 12th Ave. 604-736-5512.
www.shaughnessyvillage.com.*
At 13 storeys, this edifice southeast of downtown advertises itself as the world's largest B&B. That's a claim hard to dispute, but more significant is the fact it offers comfy housing at highly affordable rates. The rooms are compact—resembling ship's berths, with wood trim and maroon tones—but well-outfitted nonetheless, with private baths. Virtually all the facilities of a major hotel are on-site, including a swimming pool and a restaurant where an English/continental breakfast is served and is included in the room rate. A billiards room, an Internet cafe, a

HOTELS

spa and a tanning facility are also on the premises. What more could you want?

YWCA Hotel/Residence
$ **115 rooms**
733 Beatty St. 604-895-5830 or 800-663-1424. www.ywcahotel.com.
A wide variety of rooms is available in this pleasant facility in the east end of downtown, from dorm-style to small kitchenette family suites. Rooms are decorated in pastels with light-coloured wood trim. A laundry, coffee shop, parking and in-room refrigerators round out the facilities; weekly and monthly rates are available. The location is close to Chinatown and the city's stadium district. Of course, the exercise facilities here are extensive.

VANCOUVER ISLAND AND WHISTLER

Luxury

The Fairmont Château Whistler
$$$$$ **550 rooms**
4599 Château Blvd., Whistler. 604-938-8000. 800-606-8244. www.fairmont.com/whistler.
Though this hotel is one of the most upscale accommodations in Whistler, the ambience is not all palatial. The building itself, at the foot of Blackcomb Mountain, is indeed château-like, and the lobby, common areas and Wildflower restaurant are all refined and elegant. But the rooms, some outfitted in upscale country wood furniture and others in a neutral Neo-classical design, are relaxed and spacious—and virtually all have a view of snowcapped peaks. The proximity of the lifts means the Château is a ski-in, ski-out property. With a spa and golf course, this property offers complete R&R bliss.

Wickaninnish Inn
$$$$$ **76 rooms**
500 Osprey Lane, Chesterman Beach, 2mi south of Tofino. 250-725-3100 or 800-333-4604. www.wickinn.com.
When Tofino native Charles McDiarmid opened this lodge in the early 1990s, he had a radical idea: the West Coast shore could be as appealing a destination in winter as in summer. So he designed the stone-and-timber main building with huge, sturdy plate-glass windows facing the ocean, and positioned the rooms so that the winter tempests could be seen while visitors enjoyed the comforts of firelight and cosy beds. Most rooms at the Wick feature balconies facing the water; many have soaking tubs, and the style is distinctly coastal in tone and accents. The inn's spa *(see Spas)* is a destination in itself, and the **Pointe Restaurant ($$$$)** is famed for its innovative cuisine. The inn is a Relais & Châteaux member.

Expensive

🔥 The Fairmont Empress
$$$$ **477 rooms**
721 Government St., Victoria. 250-384-8111 or 866-540-4429. www.fairmont.com/empress.
Rooms in this landmark hotel *(see Excursions)* are as elegant as the building they occupy, with late Victorian and Neo-classical furnishings of walnut and brocade, spacious dimensions and every

Wickaninnish Inn

©Eric P. Lucas/Michelin

modern amenity; each room boasts a sitting area. Resplendent with fine dining, high tea *(booking in advance is highly recommended; a dress code is in place)* and a Willow Stream Spa, the Empress is the very definition of decorum. Every Victoria visitor should stay at the Empress at least once. It's best to be on a higher floor, as the street out front, Government Street, is the city's main thoroughfare, and a busy one. There's a premium on rooms facing the Inner Harbour, so you might get a better room at a more reasonable rate on the back side of the hotel. All that said, cost should be a secondary consideration—this property is one of the great hotels of the world.

Haterleigh Heritage Inn
$$$$ 6 rooms
243 Kingston St., Victoria.
250-384-9995 or 866-234-2244.
www.haterleigh.com.
The stained-glass windows in this lavish 1901 Victorian house let light pour into the lobby, awash with crystal-and-brass decorations. Most of the guest rooms have whirlpool tubs, and are furnished

with Victorian antiques, and patterned fabrics and wallpaper in keeping with the period. Breakfasts are hearty British-style affairs, with eggs, scones, pastries and sausage. Guests enjoy complimentary afternoon tea and evening sherry.

Magnolia Hotel & Spa
$$$$ 64 rooms
623 Courtney St., Victoria.
250-381-0999 or 877-624-6654.
www.magnoliahotel.com.
Opulence rules at this Old World-style boutique hotel. Mahogany walls, alabaster chandeliers and a gold gilt ceiling greet visitors in the compact lobby. All the rooms and suites are spacious, with floor-to-ceiling windows that let in ample light to complement the cream-and-beige decor. Large bathrooms have separate walk-in showers and soaking tubs. A long list of amenities ranges from a wet bar and fridge in every room to a full-service day spa in the hotel. The on-site **Prime Steakhouse ($$$)** complements the mature elegance of the hotel. The location is ideal for walking to Fort Street, Old Town, Chinatown and the Inner Harbour.

Moderate

Bedford Regency

$$$ **40 rooms**

1140 Government St., Victoria.
250-384-6835 or 800-665-6500.
www.bedfordregency.com.

Located a short walk away from the Inner Harbour and Government Street shops, this boutique hotel has handsomely appointed guest rooms with wood-burning fireplaces, large cushy chairs and goose-down duvets. Some rooms feature whirlpool tubs, flower-bedecked window boxes and views of James Bay. Pub fare is served on the premises in the English-style **Garrick's Head ($$)**.

Fairholme Manor

$$$ **6 suites**

4638 Rockland Place, Victoria.
250-598-3240 or 877-511-3322.
www.fairholmemanor.com.

This stately Italianate mansion occupies a serene, large lot atop Rockland Hill, next to Government

House. The 1885 house comprises 7,000sq ft; the two suites in the main house boast high ceilings, bay windows overlooking the garden, and expansive baths with deep tubs. Breakfast is European, but not continental—multiple courses include eggs and pastries. All rooms are suites, decorated in an understated Victorian-era manner, and with gas or wood-burning fireplaces and soaker tubs.

🏖 Long Beach Lodge Resort

$$$ **41 rooms,**
                 10 cottages

1441 Pacific Rim Hwy., Tofino.
250-725-2442 or 877-844-7873.
www.longbeachlodgeresort.com.

Warm, comfortable tones of wood dominate both the decor and the atmosphere at this beachfront lodge in Tofino. The lobby and public spaces feature huge Douglas-fir beams and trim; the exterior is cedar shake, with metal roofing and stone accents. A cheery fire crackles in the large stone fireplace indoors. Rooms are done up in handmade fir furniture, with sizable soaking tubs and balconies or patios overlooking the ocean. Amenities include small refrigerators and coffee makers. The lodge lies steps away from a mile-long broad sand beach, with enticing headlands at either end. Pacific Rim National Park Reserve lies just a few kilometres to the south. Pet-friendly, the lodge provides a BBQ shelter where guests can create their own meals, an outdoor hot tub, a sauna and exercise room, and offers surfing instruction and rentals.

Fairholme Manor

©Fairholme Manor

Long Beach Lodge Resort

©Long Beach Lodge Resort

🛏 Rosewood Victoria Inn

$$$ **17 rooms**

595 Michigan St., Victoria.
250-384-6644 or 866-986-2222.
www.viresorts.com/resorts/
Rosewood.html.

The sunny yellow exterior of this
small inn near the Parliament
Buildings hints at the cosy warmth
inside. The airy courtyard lets in
light, and the cheery wallpaper
and floral fabrics in the rooms
continue the Victorian and Colonial
theme. Each individually decorated
room has a balcony or patio; most
have fireplaces. Rates include a
four-course breakfast served in
the conservatory or out on the
heated patio.

🛏 Summit Lodge

$$$ **81 rooms**

4359 Main St., Whistler.
604-932-2778 or 888-913-8811.
www.summitlodge.com.

This low-key, expertly run boutique
hotel is ideal for travellers who
want to focus on the skiing and
golf they came to Whistler to
enjoy. The comfortable rooms have

compact kitchenettes, country
pine furniture and balconies; most
rooms offer stunning mountain
views. The service is friendly and
knowledgeable; and the location
in the middle of Whistler Village is
handy to on-mountain activities
and village life. A pool, hot tub,
sauna and spa are on the premises.
The inn is also pet-friendly.

Inexpensive

Whistler Hostel International

$ **30 rooms**

1035 Legacy Way., Whistler.
604-932-5492. www.hihostels.ca.
Located 8km south of Whistler
Village, this hostel was purpose-
built as part of the 2010 Olympics
athletes' village. It offers 108
beds in shared quarters, and 20
private rooms to members and
nonmembers alike. Amenities
include a large guest kitchen and
dining room, a media room with a
fireplace, a billiards room, a sauna,
and bicycle and ski storage. Grab
a quick meal at **Cheaky's Café ($)**
and enjoy dining on the patio.

HOTELS

VANCOUVER

INDEX

INDEX

INDEX

INDEX

INDEX

List of Maps

Photo Credits (page Icons)

Must Know
©Blackred/iStockphoto.com *Star Attractions: 6–9*
©Luckynick/Dreamstime.com *Ideas and Tours: 10–15*
©Nigel Carse/iStockphoto.com *Calendar of Events: 16–19*
©Richard Cano/iStockphoto.com *Practical Information: 20–33*

Must Sees
©City of Vancouver *Neighbourhoods: 36–43*
©canadaplace.ca *Landmarks: 44–51*
©Terraxplorer/iStockphoto.com *Museums: 52–59*
©Jessica Gnyp/Roedde House *Museum Historic Sites: 60–63*
©Scott Cramer/iStockphoto.com *Parks and Gardens: 64–73*
©Grouse Mountain *Nearby Vancouver: 74–85*
© Kutt Niinepuu/Dreamstime.com *Excursions: 86–105*

Must Dos
©Yurovskikh Aleksander/iStockphoto.com *Fun: 106–109*
©Christopher Jones/iStockphoto.com *Outdoor Fun: 110–113*
©ALEAIMAGE/iStockphoto.com *Kids: 114–117*
©Shannon Workman/Bigstockphoto.com *Performing Arts: 118–121*
©narvikk/iStockphoto.com *Shopping: 122–125*
©Jill Chen/iStockphoto.com *Nightlife: 126–129*
©Subbotina Anna/Fotolia.com *Spas: 130–133*
©Marie-France Bélanger/iStockphoto.com *Restaurants: 134–143*
©Larry Roberg/iStockphoto.com *Hotels: 144–153*